CW00520684

The Battle of Camden and the British High Tide in the South, August 16, 1780

by Robert Orrison
and Mark Wilcox

Dan Welch, series editor
Robert Orrison, chief historian

The Emerging Revolutionary War Series

offers compelling, easy-to-read overviews of some of the Revolutionary War's
most important battles and stories.

Also part of the Emerging Revolutionary War Series:

*A Single Blow: The Battles of Lexington and Concord and the Beginning of the American Revolution,
April 19, 1775* by Phillip S. Greenwalt and Robert Orrison

A Handsome Flogging: The Battle of Monmouth, June 28, 1778 by William R. Griffith IV

Victory or Death: The Battles of Trenton and Princeton, December 25, 1776–January 3, 1777
by Mary Maloy

The Winter that Won the War: The Winter Encampment at Valley Forge, 1777–1778
by Phillip S. Greenwalt

Unhappy Catastrophes: The American Revolution in Central New Jersey, 1776–1782
by Robert M. Dunkerly

To the Last Extremity: The Battles for Charleston, 1776–1782 by Mark Maloy

*For a complete list of titles in the Emerging Revolutionary War Series,
visit www.emergingrevolutionarywar.org*

The Battle of Camden and the British High Tide in the South, August 16, 1780

by Robert Orrison
and Mark Wilcox

Savas Beatie
California

© 2023 Robert Orrison and Mark Wilcox

All rights reserved. No part of this publication may be reproduced, stored in a retrieval system, or transmitted, in any form or by any means, electronic, mechanical, photocopying, recording, or otherwise, without the prior written permission of the publisher. Printed in the United States of America.

First edition, first printing

ISBN-13: 978-1-61121-686-8 (paperback)
ISBN-13: 978-1-61121-687-5 (ebook)

Names: Orrison, Robert, author. | Wilcox, Mark, 1962- author.
Title: All that can be expected : the Battle of Camden and the British high
    tide in the South, August 16, 1780 / by Robert Orrison and Mark Wilcox.
Other titles: Battle of Camden and the British high tide in the South,
    August 16, 1780
Description: El Dorado Hills, CA : Savas Beatie, [2023] | Series: Emerging
    Revolutionary War series | Includes bibliographical references. |
    Summary: "This book describes the events that led to one of the worst
    American military defeats in United States history. The authors lead you
    in the footsteps of American and British soldiers throughout the South
    Carolina backcountry. They interweave a clear historic narrative while
    guiding the reader to historic locations, creating a precise
    understanding of the events of August 1780"-- Provided by publisher.
Identifiers: LCCN 2023015807 | ISBN 9781611216868 (paperback) |
    ISBN 9781611216875 (ebook)
Subjects: LCSH: Camden, Battle of, Camden, S.C., 1780. | South
    Carolina--History--Revolution, 1775-1783. | Gates, Horatio, 1728-1806. |
    Cornwallis, Charles Cornwallis, Marquis, 1738-1805.
Classification: LCC E241.C17 O77 2023 | DDC 973.3/36--dc23/
    eng/20230607
LC record available at https://lccn.loc.gov/2023015807

SB

Published by
Savas Beatie LLC
989 Governor Drive, Suite 102
El Dorado Hills, California 95762
Phone: 916-941-6896
sales@savasbeatie.com
www.savasbeatie.com

Savas Beatie titles are available at special discounts for bulk purchases in the United States by corporations, institutions, and other organizations. For more details, you may e-mail us at sales@savasbeatie.com, or visit our website at www.savasbeatie.com for additional information.

Mark: This book is dedicated to my wonderfully supportive and encouraging wife, Kimberly.

Rob: This book is dedicated to my father Sam Orrison and my grandfather, Albert Orrison. Both men, like the Patriots of Camden, served their country, and I am forever grateful.

Table of Contents

ACKNOWLEDGMENTS   ix

TOURING THE CAROLINAS   xii

FOREWORD *by Dr. Jim Piecuch*   xv

INTRODUCTION   xxi

CHAPTER ONE: "Whatever May Be the Fate of South Carolina"
Horatio Gates Answers the Call   1

CHAPTER TWO: "Northern Laurels for Southern Willows"
Formation of Gates's Grand Army   9

CHAPTER THREE: "Before Any Thing of Consequence"
Cornwallis's Dilemma   17

CHAPTER FOUR: "Fatigued, and Almost Famished"
Gates Moves Through the Carolinas   27

CHAPTER FIVE: "An Advantageous Situation"
The Eve of Battle   39

CHAPTER SIX: "Gentlemen, What Is Best to Be Done?"
Patriot Strategy   49

CHAPTER SEVEN: "They Have Done All That Can Be Expected of Them"
The Collapse of the Continentals   61

CHAPTER EIGHT: "In This Unguarded and Critical Moment"
The Battle of Fishing Creek   71

EPILOGUE: British High Tide   81

APPENDIX A: "Their Immortal Honour Made a Brave Defense"
by Phillip Greenwalt   93

APPENDIX B: Colonial Militia *by Eric Williams*   99

APPENDIX C: Partisan Leaders *by Robert M. Dunkerly*   105

APPENDIX D: South Carolina Backcountry Summer 1780 Tour   111

APPENDIX E: Gates's Road to Camden   121

APPENDIX F: City of Camden Driving Tour   135

Table of Contents

(continued)

APPENDIX G: The Camden Burial Project *by Mark Wilcox*   147

Order of Battle   155

Suggested Reading   157

About the Authors   164

List of Maps

Maps by Edward Alexander

Southern Theater, 1780   xxiii

Gates's Road to Camden   28

The Road to Camden   34

The March to Camden   41

The Battle of Camden, Night of August 15, 1780   45

The Battle of Camden, August 16, 1780, Dawn   50

The Battle of Camden, August 16, 1780, Morning   56

Retreat from Camden   62

South Carolina Backcountry 1780 Driving Tour   112

Gates's Road to Camden Driving Tour   122

City of Camden Driving Tour   136

Footnotes for the volume are available at
https://emergingrevolutionarywar.org/emerging-revolutionary-war-series/to-the-last-extremity-footnotes/

Battle of Camden

Acknowledgments

So many people are to thank for this book. Most of all our families and friends who provided support to allow us to follow our passion and see this project through. We both would like to thank Edward Alexander for providing not just great maps, but also advice on the overall project. Editors Dan Welch and Dr. Chris Mackowski keep the "emerging" series of books going and both were instrumental in the release of this book. Also, without Ted Savas, his staff at Savas Beatie, and Patrick McCormick, none of this would be possible. Ted is one of the leaders in publishing military history. We are also grateful for those authors who contributed appendices as they added great insight to topics not covered deeply in the main text.

We are very thankful for having so many historians and experts on the Southern Campaigns read over our manuscript. Dr. John Maass is not only a good friend, but a great researcher and historian on the American Revolution. John wrote a concise history on the battle of Camden that provides a basic understanding of the battle and its consequences. He provided support and constant encouragement (always asking "you done yet?"). That kind of push is always needed. Dr. Jim Piecuch not only provided a great foreword but gave us an excellent tour of the battlefield in a pouring rainstorm. Just when we thought we were all soaked, Jim suggested we go check out the west side of the road. We found out even when you think you are soaked, you can always get wetter.

Displays in the Revolutionary War Visitor Center at Camden tell the complex story of South Carolina in the American Revolution, with a focus on the importance of Camden. (ro)

Jim is a good friend and great historian. Good friend and National Park Ranger Robert (Bert) Dunkerly, an amazing author in his own right, provided the initial inspiration for this book. Bert's intricate knowledge of the Southern Campaign, the Camden area, and his introductions to the many local historians who have been so beneficial to us were truly instrumental in helping us understand this most important chapter of the war. Rick Wise has spent countless hours leading battlefield tours at Camden and working on the Liberty Trail. Rick drove us the entire route of Gates's march from North Carolina to Camden, finding every campsite and old road trace. Rick is a great partner for anyone who is interested to learn more about South Carolina's Revolutionary War history. Archaeologists and scholars James Legg and Dr. Steven Smith provided us with a wealth of information regarding their 2022 Camden Burial Project. This includes a host of intriguing photographs of various artifacts that were recovered from the excavated graves of the 14 battle veterans

Finally, Charles Baxley and David Reuwer were instrumental not just in this book, but in the preservation and research on Camden. When I first met both men, their passion and knowledge about Camden was not just apparent, but also infectious. No one knows more about Camden than they do. Through many visits to Camden, emails, and phone calls, both were selfless in sharing information and time. These two gentlemen can easily spark a person's interest, passion and, most of all, appreciation. They inspired us to want to bring more people to this community to learn its history. If you love small town America and history, Camden is a place you need to visit.

Mark: I have been intrigued by the battle of Camden for over thirty years now, after being introduced to the story in the 1990's. My first trip to the town and to the battlefield occurred while in the company of good friends and historians, one of whom being my coauthor, Rob Orrison. I was overjoyed when Rob, already a successful and published author, asked me to join him in the writing of this book! His guidance for me during this process has been unquestionably appreciated. Many thanks to you, Rob! I would also like to thank my wonderful wife, Kimberly, for her ongoing support of my taking on these writing duties, my many road trips to South

Carolina over the last couple of years, and for always being my sounding board!

Rob: In life, we all juggle so many responsibilities and projects. In no way could I have completed this book without the support of my wife Jamie. She has put up with many research trips, nights closed off in the basement researching and writing, and helping to keep our two young boys away for a few hours so I could focus on this project. Thanks also to my co-author and good friend Mark Wilcox. I met Mark though mutual history friends that took "history trips" to Revolutionary War sites. Mark is one of the nicest people I know, always willing to help anyone out that needs it. He has proven to be a great historian and author as well. I am honored that he agreed to do this project with me. Though history is a second career for him, he has shown he has always been a historian.

PHOTO CREDITS: Chris Atkinson (ca); Dan Welch (dw); Edward Alexander (ea); Historic American Buildings Survey (habs); James Legg (jl); L. K. Scott (lks); Mark Maloy (mm); Mark Wilcox (mw); Nathan Stalvey (ns); New York City Parks and Recreation (nycpr); New York Public Library (nypl); Phillip Greenwalt (pg); Robert Dunkerly (rd); Rob Orrison (ro); Ryan Williams (rw); Sara Johnson (sj); State Archives of North Carolina (sanc)

For the Emerging Revolutionary War Series

Theodore P. Savas, *publisher*
Chris Mackowski, *advisory editor*
Dan Welch, *series editor*
Robert Orrison, *chief historian and co-founder*
Sarah Keeney, *editorial consultant*

Maps by Edward Alexander
Design and layout by Veronica Kane

Touring the Carolinas

This book serves as a historical narrative and a hands-on tour of historic sites related to the summer of 1780 in South Carolina. The best way to learn about these important events in our national history is to visit the sites where these events took place. We encourage you to take this book along with you and read it as you visit these sites. Our mission is to provide opportunities to learn about these important moments in our history where they actually happened. We also ask you to support the preservation and continued interpretation of these important sites.

There are three driving tours that focus on the Camden campaign. The first tour will focus on some of the sites associated with the partisan fighting in South Carolina in the summer of 1780. Many of these sites are part of the Liberty Trail, a collaborative effort to connect South Carolina's American Revolutionary War sites. The second tour will take readers on Gates's route from North Carolina to Camden with various important stops. The final tour is a tour of the town of Camden and Historic Camden. There are also self-guided walking tours available at Historic Camden and the Camden battlefield. In 2023, the Camden battlefield underwent many improvements expanding visitor access, trails, and interpretation.

As you take these tours, please drive safely, obey traffic laws, and respect private property. Many of the sites we take you to on these tours are exclusive sites that are on private property; please do not trespass and stay in the public right of way when visiting these locations. As you visit, think about those in

1780 that marched many of these same routes and fought over this ground. Most were hundreds (some thousands!) of miles away from home. Their sacrifice was the foundation for our country and a government of the governed.

Note on Terminology Used In This Book

Throughout the book we use the terms "Whigs," "Americans," and "Patriots" to describe those who were fighting for the cause of American independence. (Most Americans at the time identified more with their states, and armies were often composed of diverse arrays of people from different countries.) Continental forces refer to those professionally enlisted into the service of the United States of America. These men were professional and paid soldiers, as opposed to militia that were unprofessional fighting forces raised by the states for limited service. Many Americans also sided with the Crown forces, and we describe these men as "Loyalists" or "Tories," even though many of them also saw themselves as patriots.

For the Crown forces, we use the term "British," even though large portions of their army included Irish, American, and German soldiers. Provincial forces describe enlisted soldiers in the British army that were American born. These men were recruited from the colonies and were uniformed in the British service. Often they were grouped into their own units. We use these terms for simplicity and style reasons.

$\mathcal{F}$oreword

BY DR. JIM PIECUCH

Despite its importance, the battle of Camden, fought on August 16, 1780, eight miles north of its namesake town in South Carolina, has until recently received scant attention from historians and the public, who preferred to focus on American victories and events where George Washington was present. This neglect is unfortunate, as the battle was one of the Revolutionary War's most important engagements. When Lieutenant General Charles, Earl Cornwallis's 2,200 British troops clashed with General Horatio Gates's roughly 4,000 American soldiers at dawn in the open pine forest, the fate of the southern states hung in the balance. Barely an hour later, the American army had been nearly annihilated. British cavalrymen pursued its remnants northward while their counterparts in the infantry rounded up hundreds of prisoners. The British conquest of the southern states seemed certain.

The repercussions of the battle were felt far and wide. In the fledgling United States, the disaster shook generals, governors, and members of the Continental Congress. Barely three months earlier, the British had captured an entire American army at Charleston and occupied South Carolina. Now a second army, including eight regiments of veteran Continental troops, had been shattered, with the loss of all its artillery and equipment. North Carolina lay open to invasion, with only part-time, poorly trained militia soldiers to defend it, and most of the North Carolina militiamen who fought at Camden, and all the Virginians, had fled at the first sight of British

The Great Wagon Road was a primary route of settlement of the American south in the "back country." Today, vestiges of the Great Wagon Road can be seen in old road traces through the Camden battlefield. (ro)

bayonets. Horatio Gates, of whom much had been expected—he was, after all, the "Hero of Saratoga" who had captured an entire British army in 1777— had suffered irreparable damage to his reputation. He was swept off the battlefield while trying to rally the fleeing militia, and afterward he made the justifiable, but ill-advised, decision to ride to Hillsborough to seek assistance from the North Carolina legislature, making it appear as though he had fled over 180 miles from the battlefield in three days. He would soon be removed from command.

The disaster also affected ordinary people, who wondered about the fate of their loved ones. The confusion after the battle was so great that American officers were never able to determine their exact number of casualties, and hundreds of soldiers were simply listed as missing. Family members pressed governors to get information about what had happened to their husbands, sons, and brothers. Some survivors straggled into Charlotte in the days following the battle, others were later reported captured, but many were never accounted for. The impact of the tragedy cannot be understated.

In Europe, responses varied. French officials worried that, having invested so much money and manpower to assist their American allies, they had made a grave mistake. From Holland, John Adams complained that his prospects of securing a loan from the Dutch had greatly diminished after news of Camden reached that country. The reaction was far different in London, where British leaders believed they had finally gotten the upper hand in suppressing the American rebellion. Thus, the shots fired at Camden that August morning, like those more famously fired in Massachusetts on April 19, 1775, and commemorated in verse, were truly "heard round the world."

If the Revolutionary cause in the South had truly suffered a devastating blow at Camden, and it had, then why didn't a final, decisive British victory follow? There were many reasons, some of which began to be visible soon after the battle. The governments of North Carolina and Virginia, realizing the threat they faced, made greater exertions to get troops in the field and properly supply them. South Carolinians and Georgians drew hope from the fact that the Continental Congress had sent an army to assist them. Before they learned that Gates was approaching, many people believed that Congress was going to "write off" the southern states after the loss of Charleston, and were prepared to accept, however grudgingly, British rule. Gates's attempt to drive out the British convinced many that Congress would not abandon them, and they decided to resist the occupying forces. As Lt. Col. Francis, Lord Rawdon, who commanded the British left wing at Camden noted, Gates's advance ignited an uprising that caught British commanders by surprise. Partisan leaders like Francis Marion and Thomas Sumter had already been resisting the British; after Camden, their forces grew, and they harassed British outposts and lines of communication, tying down substantial numbers of Cornwallis's troops.

Cornwallis also contributed, unintentionally, to the reversal of American fortunes. He was not prepared to follow up his victory at Camden. He spent the next several weeks preparing to invade North Carolina, and when he did advance in September, he got only as far as Charlotte, where he found his army surrounded and harassed by partisans. While he pondered his next move, the left wing of his invasion force, consisting primarily of Loyalist militia, was virtually annihilated at Kings Mountain by Revolutionary militia on October 7. The blow forced Cornwallis to retreat to South Carolina, where he continued to be vexed by partisans until January 1781, when after another disastrous defeat at Cowpens, he set off across North Carolina in pursuit of the reconstituted Continental Army, a trek that would ultimately lead him to Virginia and his surrender at Yorktown in October.

In this volume, Rob Orrison and Mark Wilcox not only give the battle of Camden the attention it deserves, they also provide a guide to touring the battlefield and important sites related to the battle. There is no better way to understand the events of the past than to follow them "on the ground," and Rob and Mark have enabled readers to do just that, whether in the form of personal visits to the sites, or from the comfort of their armchairs as they read this important story from America's struggle for independence.

*JIM PIECUCH **earned his BA and MA degrees at the University of New Hampshire and his PhD at the College of William & Mary. He is a former history professor and has written several articles on colonial and Revolutionary history. He is also the author of several books focusing on the American Revolution in the south, including** The Battle of Camden: A Documentary History **(History Press, 2006).***

"The Ground on which the armies
met was not the choice of the
general but the accident of the night."
—William Davies

Introduction

In the spring of 1780, the prospects of British success in the southern colonies were looking up. Most of Georgia was under British control, and the joint military venture of American and French forces to retake Savannah in the fall of 1779 had failed. Seeking to end the stalemate between American and British forces in the north, British Lieut. Gen. Sir Henry Clinton (also serving as overall commander of all British forces in North America) decided to dedicate nearly 15,000 British soldiers and sailors to capture one of the largest cities in the colonies: Charles Town (Charleston), South Carolina. The hope was that the population in the south was favorable to the British cause, and Loyalist leaders in the south promised a strong turnout of military support from the population. Up to this point in the conflict, these Loyalist leaders had delivered on these promises. Clinton had great success in filling regiments with Loyalists in New York and New Jersey. Also, the southern colonies were providing men and material for the war effort in the north and, by taking the war south, Clinton hoped to cut off the lifeline for George Washington's army in the north.

Working closely with the Royal Navy under Adm. Mariot Arbuthnot, Clinton was determined to learn from previous failed attempts to capture Charleston. His objective was to land his army south of the city, swing them westward, and approach Charleston from the west. By using tried and true siege tactics in which his professional army was well trained, Clinton aimed to lay siege to the city, capturing it and the American

The battle of Waxhaws monument was placed in 1860 over the mass grave of 84 American soldiers, the obelisk today is mostly unreadable. In 1955, a new monument was located nearby with the original inscription. Another grave nearby contains 25 other men who died after the battle. (ro)

Lieutenant General Sir
Henry Clinton became the
commander-in- chief of
all Crown forces in North
America on February 4, 1778.
Clinton was immediately
hampered by having to send
nearly 5,000 men to the
Caribbean to reinforce British
efforts there. (nypl)

Major General Benjamin
Lincoln was put in a hard
position in the spring of 1780.
His small army was vastly
outnumbered by Clinton's
forces and he had no navy
to speak of to confront the
British fleet. City leaders
in Charleston told him if he
moved the Continental Army
out of the city's defenses, they
would tip off the British and
let them in the city. (nypl)

army stationed there. Commanded by Maj. Gen. Benjamin Lincoln, the Continental force defending Charleston was the largest American army south of Pennsylvania. Lincoln was not only responsible for Charleston, but also the entire southern colonies. Within a month and a half, Clinton had Lincoln bottled up in Charleston with nowhere to go, with Arbuthnot blocking the harbor. Going against his own best judgment, Lincoln did not take a chance to evacuate the city with his army, fearing city leaders would open the gates to the British before he left. In a no-win situation, on May 12, 1780, Lincoln surrendered 5,500 soldiers and sailors and nearly 300 cannon. It was one of the worst American defeats of the war. Clinton granted parole to the militia, but of the nearly 2,500 Continental soldiers many were sent to the hulks of prison ships in the harbor. These were some of the worst prisoner conditions of the war, and many perished that summer.

With the largest city in the south in British hands, Clinton believed that all he had to do was establish outposts in South Carolina stationed with British Regulars. This he believed would put down what was left of the rebellion in the state. These posts assisted the recruitment and training of the thousands of Loyalist troops he believed would now rally around the King's Colors. To take the best advantage of his Regular troops, Clinton determined to establish three major outposts in the South Carolina backcountry. Clinton established these posts at Augusta (Georgia), Ninety Six, and Camden. While these posts were to be centers for the British army, the local Loyalist militias were to serve as the pacification forces in South Carolina while the main British force was freed up for larger strategic goals.

To recruit, enlist, and train the large, expected influx of Loyalist militia, Clinton named Maj. Patrick Ferguson as Inspector of Militia. Ferguson was ordered to enlist younger men, preferably unmarried, into companies that would form battalions. He was instructed to recruit from Georgia to North Carolina and offer short enlistments if necessary. Clinton believed that having the colonists maintain their own law and order (via Great Britain's authority) would cause less apprehension with those that were mostly undecided about to whom they should throw their support, the Patriots or the British.

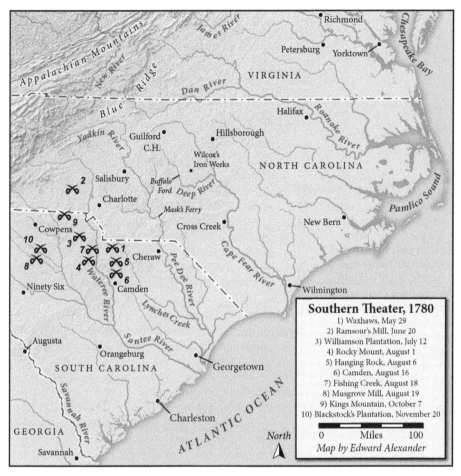

SOUTHERN THEATER, 1780—Southern military operations during the American Revolutionary War.

By mid-May, the British army set out for their destinations in the back country. Clinton's second in command, Lt. Gen. Charles Lord Cornwallis, marched to Camden while Ferguson moved to Ninety Six. Without much resistance, Clinton's plan to conquer South Carolina was working perfectly. Patriot leaders scrambled to find ways to organize their resistance. The only organized Continental force remaining in South Carolina was a small force of Virginians under Col. Abraham Buford that was on its way to Charleston when the city surrendered. He was ordered by Brig. Gen. Isaac Huger to reverse course and make his way north toward Hillsborough, North Carolina. There, along with the North Carolina militia, he could be the core of American defense in North Carolina.

Charleston on the eve of the American Revolution was thriving and ringed with defenses built by the British to protect the harbor from the French, Spanish, and pirates. The city was diverse with a wide variety of ethnic groups immigrating to the area. Charleston's economy relied heavily on African slave labor, serving as one of the largest slave trading ports in America. (nypl)

Founded in 1670 as "Charles Town" in honor of King Charles II, Charleston sat in an ideal position at the confluence of the Ashley and Cooper Rivers in a natural harbor along the Atlantic Ocean. The current location replaced a nearby settlement with the same name in 1680. The city quickly became the fifth largest port in North America by 1690. (nypl)

On May 27, Cornwallis ordered Lt. Col. Banastre Tarleton with 300 of his dragoons and mounted infantry in pursuit of Buford. Tarleton's British Legion was mostly composed of Loyalist recruits, so many in his force were from America. Tarleton pushed his men and horses hard, many horses falling out along the way. Buford was aware of a possible British pursuit but underestimated the speed in which Tarleton closed the gap. On May 29, Tarleton caught up with Buford in a region near the South and North Carolina border called the "Waxhaws."

The events that took place next are still debated today. Tarleton under a flag of truce tried to get Buford to surrender. Writing to Buford, Tarleton wrote "Resistance being vain, to prevent the effusion of human blood, I make offers which can never be repeated." Tarleton was already creating an image of himself as an aggressive and brutal fighter. Buford, however, refused, replying, "I reject your proposals, and shall defend myself to the last extremity." With that, Buford continued his march north towards North Carolina as did Tarleton's pursuit. Around 3:00 p.m., the lead elements of Tarleton's force wiped out Buford's small rearguard, forcing Buford to stop and deal with Tarleton.

Buford decided to create a single battle line east of the Rocky River Road. Tarleton, ever the aggressive commander, ordered his horsemen to charge the Virginians. Here, Buford made what would be a devastating blunder. He ordered his men to not fire until the British cavalry was within ten yards of the American line. This would not allow the Americans a chance to fire another volley before the British

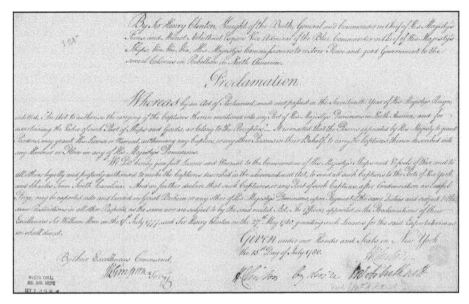

charge was upon them. The Virginians fired, taking out some of the British dragoons and horses (Tarleton himself became briefly trapped under his horse), but most charged through Buford's line, wielding their sabers and cutting down the Virginians. Total chaos ensued, and many of Buford's men attempted to flee. Some tried to surrender by throwing their arms to the ground, but American accounts state that the British were offering "no quarter" and killing everyone that tried to surrender. Other accounts report that Buford sent a white flag to Tarleton, but probably because he was injured, it was never received, and the fighting continued. Accounts differ widely between the Americans and British on the fighting, but the fact cannot be argued that Buford's command was destroyed.

American casualties were estimated at 350: 113 men killed, 147 wounded, 50 captured, and 2 six-pound artillery pieces and 26 wagons captured. Buford himself was able to escape the field. Tarleton only suffered 5 killed and 12 wounded, a complete victory. What has become known as "Buford's Massacre" was not referred to as a massacre at all in many period accounts. Tarleton himself blamed the "slaughter" on the fact that his men thought he was killed in the battle and sought revenge. The disparity in numbers and the reports of indiscriminate British slaughter of Americans led to the creation of "Tarleton's Quarter." Patriot leaders quickly pounced on this and began to

Clinton issued several proclamations before he left South Carolina. One of the most influential was his June 3 Proclamation in which he retracted his lenient policy toward those who pledged their loyalty to the King. Clinton declared that all South Carolina residents needed to pledge their loyalty within seventeen days or they would be considered rebel combatants. Cornwallis was blindsided by Clinton's proclamations, which made his job to bring South Carolina under control that much harder. (nypl)

Lt. Col. Banastre Tarleton is still one of the most recognizable figures of the American Revolution. His ability to strike with ferocity with men recruited from the colonies made him a hated man among the Patriots. (nypl)

Tarleton's outnumbered mounted legion made quick work of the American infantry. Buford's mistake of holding his men's fire until the cavalry was right on top of them was a major cause of the American disaster. It was one of the most lopsided victories of the American Revolution. (nypl)

spread stories about Tarleton's brutal tactics. This proved to be a public relations coup for the Patriot cause, as it energized their side and led to a more robust recruitment of militia and partisan forces to take on the British, who now faced no organized opposition in South Carolina or Georgia.

On June 8, Clinton sailed back to New York with nearly 4,000 men of his army and left Cornwallis in command in the south. The relationship between Clinton and Cornwallis was much strained, and Cornwallis was willing to serve anywhere that was not with Clinton. If this had to be in the south, so be it, but Cornwallis soon discovered that total victory in the Carolinas was not such a sure thing. Cornwallis established the planned outposts across Georgia and South Carolina at Augusta, Georgia and Ninety Six and Camden in South Carolina. Operating out of these posts, Cornwallis hoped he could provide supplies to his Regulars, as well as recruit Loyalist militia to help him keep control of the region while he took the bulk of his army northward into North Carolina. Though Cornwallis never had much faith in Loyalist militias.

Before leaving Charleston, Clinton decided to issue several proclamations, each changing the intent of the previous one. The first proclamation on May 22 took a hard line in dealing with Patriot militia and political supporters. Contradicting the terms offered to Lincoln's army at the surrender of Charleston (allowing the militia and civilians to be paroled and go home without serving as prisoners of war), Clinton wrote that anyone taking up arms against the British government or encouraging others to do so would be subject to imprisonment and having their property confiscated by British authorities. Ten days later Clinton issued another proclamation, offering full pardons to all who pledged their allegiance to the Crown, requiring people to pledge their loyalty to avoid harassment. Finally, on June 3, Clinton issued his most incendiary proclamation. This time Clinton required that all parolees had to sign an oath of allegiance within seventeen days, or they would be considered rebel combatants by British forces and officials.

There were no neutrals in the fight in South Carolina; you were either with or against the Crown.

THE BATTLE OF THE WAXHAWS, MAY 29TH, 1780.

As word quickly spread after the May 29 defeat of Buford's men, Patriot leaders used the event as a propaganda tool. "Tarleton's Quarter" was heard across the south and angered many Americans who were not yet committed. Though the casualties were lopsided, new research shows that most of the "massacre" accounts were made many years after the war. (nypl)

This action forced people to either choose a side or take the oath of allegiance to avoid harassment. Many who did end up fighting with the Patriots anyways. Colonel Francis Lord Rawdon noted the negative impacts of these proclamations on the population in the back country in a letter to Cornwallis. "That unfortunate proclamation of the 3rd of June has had very unfavorable consequences," he wrote. "The majority of the inhabitants in the frontier districts, tho' ill-disposed to us, from circumstances were not actually in arms against us." As Rawdon pointed out, the Clinton proclamations forced everyone to take sides, when many would have preferred to stay neutral. Rawdon and Cornwallis soon saw the impact as the Patriot militias began to gain more members.

Cornwallis realized quickly how difficult it would be to maintain control of Georgia and South Carolina while trying to subdue North Carolina. He faced not only limited forces in his rank and file, but also insufficient arms. This was compounded by the accidental explosion of a powder magazine in Charleston that destroyed thousands of pounds of black powder, firearms, and killed hundreds. Cornwallis also realized he lacked the political leadership amongst Royal officials to operate the newly reconstituted government of the Crown. Cornwallis was a better commander in the field than he was a political leader in heading a government. It became apparent that, due to many factors, South Carolina would not be as easily held as Clinton had thought. Now Cornwallis not only had to plan for an invasion of North Carolina to continue the British subjugation of the south, but he also had to find a way to deal with partisans in South Carolina who were organizing and becoming very effective in opposing Crown rule.

"Whatever May Be the Fate of South Carolina"

Horatio Gates Answers the Call

CHAPTER ONE

By the spring of 1780, American Major General Horatio Gates was frustrated with his lack of involvement in the war. Surely he deserved a more prominent place in the field, not serving behind a desk in Boston or Albany. Relying on his many friends in Congress, Gates lobbied for command of the Southern Department. His friend John Mathews, Congressman from South Carolina, shared Gates's wishes with his colleagues, but to no avail. In frustration, Mathews wrote Gates "whatever may be the fate of South Carolina . . . I have done my duty to my Country, by pointing out in time the means for its preservation."

Horatio Gates was born in Essex, England in 1727. His father worked in the British Customs Service and his mother served as the head housekeeper for the Duke of Bolton. This tertiary connection to high society provided the Gates family some opportunity and the ability to expose a young Horatio Gates to a good education. With assistance from his parents, Gates was able to purchase a military commission (which was the custom of the time for officers) with the 20th Regiment of Foot. Gates served admirably as a solider through the War of Austrian Succession, then was promoted to the rank of captain while serving in Nova Scotia. He served as aide-to-camp to Lt. Gen. Edward Cornwallis (uncle to future British General Charles, Lord Cornwallis).

Gates purchased a captaincy commission in a New York Independent Company (a British company).

Near here at Berry's Ferry along the Shenandoah River, Maj. Gen. Horatio Gates convinced Daniel Morgan to return to the Continental service and join him with the Southern Army. Unfortunately, Morgan did not join Gates until after the battle of Camden. Today, the Virginia Route 7 bridge crosses the Shenandoah River at the ferry site. (ns)

Traveller's Rest was the home of Horatio Gates after he immigrated to Virginia from England. Gates knew the area well, having served with many Virginians in the French and Indian War. Gates quickly became a leader in the community as a justice and colonel of the local militia. Today, the home still stands near Kearneysville, WV, and is a private residence. (rw)

He served in the ill-fated Braddock expedition of 1755 to capture the French outpost of Fort Duquesne. Many other future leaders from the American Revolution also were with Braddock, such as George Washington, Daniel Morgan, Charles Lee, and Thomas Gage. Gates was wounded in the slaughter of the British force, but survived the campaign and served on various staffs throughout the French and Indian War. By the end of the war, Gates became frustrated as he continued to face an uphill battle for promotion, as he was neither wealthy nor well connected. Like many, he sought his fortunes in the new American colonies and purchased farmland in the northern reaches of the Shenandoah Valley of Virginia in 1772.

By the time of Lexington and Concord in 1775, Gates was committed to the Patriots' cause and offered himself to the fledging American army. As a professional military officer, George Washington recommended him as the Adjutant General of the Continental Army, to which he was appointed that June. Gates's experience as an administrator proved invaluable to the newly created army. He served in various administrative posts but longed for a field command, for which he constantly lobbied Congress. His ambition put him at odds with Washington and his supporters, and his outward jealousy of Washington's military position was a constant issue for Gates that strained their relationship. In 1776, Gates was given command of the Canadian Department (including forces under Benedict Arnold) and by 1777, he was able to use his connections in Congress to replace Gen. Phillip Schuyler as commander of the Northern Department and the field army being created to confront the British advance down the Hudson River from Canada under British General John Burgoyne.

Gates's victory over Burgoyne has been considered by many the turning point of the American Revolution. Leading the Northern American Army in New York to victory at Saratoga, he oversaw the complete destruction of a British army, forcing Burgoyne to surrender nearly 7,000 men on October 17, 1777. The victory stunned the British and convinced an already willing French monarchy to ally with the newly formed United States in their ongoing fight with Great Britain. Gates's role in the victory has been debated since 1777, but he was the American commander on the field and earned the praise from Congress.

After Saratoga, Gates looked for more military glory and believed he was the most qualified man in America to lead the Continental Army. His constant criticisms of Washington made him unpopular with Washington's supporters in Congress and most officers in the Continental Army. His rift with Benedict Arnold also helped in his unpopularity among many of the men in the army. Gates's feelings toward Washington became public during what has been called the "Conway Cabal." Letters criticizing Washington's leadership and the course of the war between Brig. Gen. Thomas Conway and Gates were made public. Supposed meetings among Gates, Conway, and other officers to remove Washington were reportedly held in York, Pennsylvania. The "cabal" galvanized support for Washington and began

The surrender of General Burgoyne's British army at Saratoga was a major turning point of the American Revolution. From the victory, Maj. Gen. Horatio Gates was lauded as a hero and became a favorite of many in Congress. Through this popularity, Gates sought and received an independent command by leading the reconstituted Southern Army. (nypl)

Based off of young George Washington's advice, Great Britain sent General Edward Braddock to North America with a force of more than 2,000 men to claim the Forks of the Ohio. On July 9, 1755, this force was surprised by a mixed force of French and Indians, leading to a disaster for the British and the death of Braddock himself. It was one of the worst defeats in the 18th century for Great Britain. (nypl)

a campaign by Washington's inner circle to punish Gates for his role. Gates apologized to Washington, but the damage was done.

Though Gates longed for an independent field command, he accepted the appointment of the Northern Department to look after the New York Highlands and watch for British incursions from Canada or New York City. Gates was unhappy in this role and proposed another American invasion of Canada. Washington and Congress disagreed and rejected his plans. He disliked his task of dealing with enemy native tribes in the region and dragged his feet in following orders. Finally, that fall, Gates took command of American forces in New England with his headquarters in Boston. Though excited by this appointment, he quickly realized that this post was not where the action would be. The British left Boston in 1776, and since that time, the city was peaceful and not a welcome place for a man seeking glory and military action. Finally, after much frustration, Gates asked to return to his farm in Virginia and arrived there by December 1779. Gates found himself a hero without an army and continued to brood over his situation.

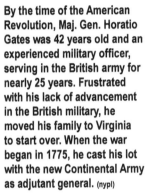

By the time of the American Revolution, Maj. Gen. Horatio Gates was 42 years old and an experienced military officer, serving in the British army for nearly 25 years. Frustrated with his lack of advancement in the British military, he moved his family to Virginia to start over. When the war began in 1775, he cast his lot with the new Continental Army as adjutant general. (nypl)

Daniel Morgan was the prototypical frontiersman. Born in New Jersey, he migrated to the Shenandoah Valley of Virginia and made a successful living as a teamster. He served along Daniel Boone in the French and Indian War and was with Braddock at his defeat along the Monongahela. He had a reputation as someone that didn't back down from a fight. (nypl)

An English born officer, Charles Lee served in the British Army as a lieutenant colonel during the French and Indian War and then a major general in the Polish army. In 1773, he moved to Virginia and became a strong supporter of colonial opposition to Crown policies. He became a good friend of George Washington before the war but became jealous of Washington's rank and influence during the war. (nypl)

Opportunity knocked for Horatio Gates with the fall of Charleston, South Carolina in May 1780. A devastating loss for the Americans, nearly 6,000 men of the Southern Army under Benjamin Lincoln surrendered to Sir Henry Clinton. Unless something was done soon, the entire southern colonies could fall and the revolution along with it. Congress needed someone who inspired men to join the war effort, and a trusted leader with a positive record. Washington put Nathanael Greene's name forward, but Congress in a rare move went against Washington's wishes and appointed Horatio Gates as commander of the Southern Department on June 13. Finally, Gates received the field command he longed for; he held one of the most important commands in America, and was far enough away from Washington to operate with some independence. Gates received the much-coveted authority he thought he deserved. In his orders, he was given freedom to call any militia from any state south of Pennsylvania. He could appoint all his officers and staff, and could draw up to $30,000

Saratoga was built in 1779 by Daniel Morgan while on a "break" in service. Morgan named the house in honor of the victory at Saratoga where he played a major role. The house was not far from Gates's home at Traveller's Rest and the two men stayed in touch while Morgan was here. When Gates was named commander of the Southern Army, one of the first persons he reached out to was Morgan. (nypl)

from the Continental treasury to pay for any of his expenses. Plus, Gates was to report to Congress and the Board of War (the de facto Department of War), bypassing Washington's authority.

Gates received word of his appointment while at his farm Traveller's Rest a few days later. He quickly made his plans and started south. But before he joined his new army, he wanted to deliver some good news to an old friend, Daniel Morgan. The two men met at Berry's Tavern in Ashby's Gap on June 28. Morgan was serving out his semi-retirement at his home a few miles west of the tavern. The two men respected one another; Morgan was still unhappy for not receiving a promotion to brigadier general the year before. Though he was unhappy with Congress, he was itching to get back into the war. He believed Gates would have success in the south and wanted to join him. Gates needed men he trusted, and secured a promotion for Morgan to lead a light infantry unit. Morgan accepted and headed home to make arrangements. Sadly for Gates, his favorite subordinate did not join him until the fall. This remains one of the many "what ifs" of the Camden campaign.

After leaving Morgan, Gates headed to Fredericksburg and then south to Richmond to meet with Governor Thomas Jefferson. Gates called on Jefferson to provide supplies, militia, and money from the state treasury to help support his army. Gates was empowered by Congress to seek out support from the states directly, without consulting George Washington or the Board of War. This was a rare luxury for Continental officers. By July 13, Gates was in Hillsborough; after writing more missives to Congress and the governors of Virginia and North Carolina, Gates set off southward. His destination was Deep River, where Continental forces from Maryland and Delaware under Maj. Gen. Baron Johann de Kalb were encamped while awaiting a department commander. De Kalb was sent south by Washington to assist the Americans in Charleston. On their way south, de Kalb received word of the fall of Charleston. These men now served as the nucleus for the new Southern Army, which Gates called his "Grand Army."

"Northern Laurels for Southern Willows"

Formation of Gates's Grand Army

CHAPTER TWO

Major General Baron Johann de Kalb arrived in America in 1777 with the Marquis de Lafayette. De Kalb was a mentor to Lafayette and was to assist him in finding his place in America. Both men wanted to assist the American colonists in their war against Great Britain. De Kalb was born in Prussia and served a life in the military. He fought in the War of Austrian Succession and then as a lieutenant colonel in the French Army during the Seven Years War (French and Indian War). He fought with distinction and received the Royal Order of Merit. There are many complexities surrounding his title of "baron." De Kalb was appointed Baron and brigadier general for the colonies by various French courtiers, undoubtedly with the knowledge and secret consent of the French Minister of War, Comte de St. Germain and the French Foreign Affairs Department under Comte de Vergennes. Most likely the French King Louis XVI himself had knowledge of the arrangement. This provided de Kalb with status and gravitas with the Continental Congress. No matter his title, de Kalb was a leader and a fighter.

De Kalb was sympathetic to the Patriot cause. During the French and Indian War, he traveled the colonies as an observer for the French to gauge the colonists' temperature for a possible revolution against Great Britain. The French hoped to regain their territory lost to Great Britain and saw the American colonies as possible future allies. During his time, de

On these fields around Cox's Mills, de Kalb encamped his small army of Maryland and Delaware Continentals. De Kalb felt this was the best location for his army to await reinforcements and supplies from the north via Hillsborough and to be close enough to South Carolina to threaten British movements there. Today, only ruins of the mills remain and the fields once bustling with soldiers have returned to quiet meadows. (ro)

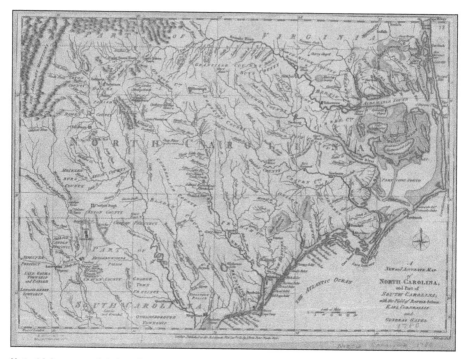

Not widely as populated as the mid Atlantic or New England states, few good roads existed in the Carolinas away from the eastern seaboard. The British authorities in London ignorantly believed that this part of North America was receptive to returning to British authority and they could turn the tide of the war here in the south. (nypl)

Kalb became charmed by the Americans and their spirit for liberty and democratic rule. De Kalb earned the respect of the British as well. Banastre Tarleton called de Kalb "an officer of reputation, who pressed forward with the troops with indefatigable attention." The German born military officer now found himself moving southward from Pennsylvania with two brigades of Washington's best troops, Maryland and Delaware Continental soldiers. De Kalb was ordered to move with speed to assist the American force under siege in Charleston under Maj. Gen. Benjamin Lincoln. On his way south, de Kalb learned that Lincoln surrendered on May 12, 1780.

With limited forces under his command (1,500 rank and file), de Kalb decided to meet with Virginia Governor Thomas Jefferson about what Virginia could do to support his men. Jefferson promised as many Virginia militia as he could muster, but warned that Virginia was already bare from supplying both the northern and southern armies. De Kalb was very frustrated by the response of Virginia officials, writing, "I meet with no support, no integrity, and no virtue in the State of Virginia." The situation in the south was now on the precipice of tragedy. There was no organized American force in the field except for partisan groups. De Kalb decided to move southward to North Carolina and hope that the Virginia and North Carolina militia would rally around his Continentals. De Kalb was delayed in his movement south by having to gather supplies and beg for currency, as well as constantly being short of the necessary wagons and horses. By July 6, de Kalb ordered his men to encamp at Buffalo Ford along the Deep River. The lack of supplies and the exertion of the men forced him to move no farther south. Sergeant William Seymour of the Delaware troops wrote the officers "could scarce keep the troops from starving, which occasioned a vast number of men to desert to the enemy."

De Kalb found that North Carolina was no more hospitable than Virginia. De Kalb's deputy adjutant general, Lt. Col. Otho Holland Williams, called Hillsborough a "dirty, disagreeable hole." Though the North Carolina government promised provisions, little came into the camp. De Kalb also called for the North Carolina militia that was now emboldened under the command of former Governor and now militia Maj. Gen. Richard Caswell to join him along Deep Creek. After several messages, Caswell refused to join de Kalb in what was a frustrating command situation for the Continentals. Furthermore, Caswell's men were out gathering supplies themselves, with little organization or procedure. De Kalb was worried that Caswell's militia, now posted along the Yadkin River, were too exposed and were vulnerable to British attack. The militia seemed more concerned with chasing Loyalists in the region rather than focusing on creating a new Southern Army to take on Cornwallis. De Kalb

Richard Caswell was a politician turned military figure and North Carolina's first state governor, serving from 1776-1780. He also spent time in North Carolina's colonial legislature as well as the First Continental Congress. Caswell was in command of North Carolina forces at the battle of Moore's Creek Bridge on February 27, 1776. (ncsa)

Tryon Palace in New Bern, North Carolina, served as the home of the Royal Governor and North Carolina colonial legislature. In 1776, Richard Caswell served as the first elected governor of North Carolina and moved into Tryon Palace. Today, the palace is rebuilt and serves as a museum focusing on North Carolina's colonial and revolutionary history. (ro)

By 1780, Thomas Jefferson left the Continental Congress and served as the governor of Virginia. Jefferson found it very difficult to be a war-time governor and constantly struggled to recruit men for the military and gather supplies for the southern army. (nypl)

always gave little credit to the militia in America, and his experience with Caswell confirmed his beliefs.

The South Carolina that laid ahead of the Continental forces was the "back country." The state was divided traditionally into three regions. The "low country" was centered along the Atlantic coast and the tidal areas. This area, first settled, had the prevalent concentration of large plantations and commercial wealth. These plantations relied heavily on slave labor, and those in the tidal areas produced highly profitable crops such as newly introduced rice and indigo.

The "back country" (or the piedmont) included the area generally 50 miles west of the coast, consisting of the districts of Camden and Ninety Six. This region of South Carolina was less settled and consisted mostly of small farms and widely dispersed towns and villages (the largest being Camden and Ninety Six). Scots Irish settlers along with some German and Scots dominated the area, and few had much affection for the larger plantation owners in the "low country." The "back country" land was mostly flat, with small hills rising westward to the Appalachians. In the area above the fall line, the land became rocky with small hills rising westward to the Appalachians. Much of the area was covered in long leaf pine forests, with little undergrowth other than wiregrass.

The people in this region were considered less "civilized" and were more inclined to violence, excessive drinking, and rough-housing. Almost all males had experience in shooting, fishing, and living outdoors. British officer Maj. George Hanger pejoratively wrote that the people of the "back country," "are more savage than the Indians and possess every one of their vices but not one of their virtues. I have known one of these fellows travel two hundred miles through the woods, never keeping any road or path, guided by the sun by day and the stars by night, to kill a particular person belonging to the opposite party."

De Kalb was in no hurry to move forward, though South Carolinian leaders called on him to relieve the pressure on Patriot partisans fighting on their own against the British. The Americans had no plans (nor the manpower) to take on the British along the coast and at Charleston. The focus was thus on Camden, a British outpost. Taking the outpost and town would relieve the northeast portion of the state, clear the way into the central North Carolina region, and isolate the

The British outpost at Ninety Six was part of Clinton and Cornwallis's plan to establish a system of posts to provide a military presence across South Carolina. Located approximately 100 miles west of Camden, the British forces in Ninety Six relied on a stockade fort (pictured) and an earthen star-shaped fort to protect the village and military post. (rd)

other British outpost at Ninety Six. The only problem was, de Kalb did not have the manpower or resources to move into South Carolina.

Though de Kalb served as the de facto Southern Department commander, he desired for another leader to take command. That man, Horatio Gates, arrived on July 25. Baron de Kalb was happy to receive Gates; he knew the situation in the south was dire and hoped that the hero of Saratoga could reenergize the Patriot cause in the Carolinas. De Kalb provided as much pomp and circumstance for Gates as his little force could. As Otho Holland Williams wrote, "the baron ordered a continental salute from the little park of artillery."

Though Gates dubbed his new Southern army his "Grand Army," there was hardly anything grand about it. The core of his army was the 1,500 rank and file crack troops of the Maryland and Delaware Lines sent south from Morristown, New Jersey, by General Washington. The brigade had gained a reputation as hard fighters since the New York campaign in 1776. Also encamped along Deep River was a small cavalry force under Col. Charles Armand. This was the core of Gates's cavalry, as most other Patriot cavalry were recuperating in Halifax from their disastrous encounters with Tarleton in the Charleston campaign. There was also the North Carolina militia under Caswell that were encamped along the Yadkin River. Though de Kalb and now Gates called on Caswell to join him, the stubborn North Carolinian still did not budge. Gates was worried his inexperienced militia were an inviting target for the British in Camden and he could ill afford to lose them. Also marching to join Gates was a large contingent of Virginia militia under

Major General Johann von Robais, Baron de Kalb was born in 1721 near Erlangen, Principality of Bayreuth (then part of the Holy Roman Empire). Though most today consider him a "German" officer, Germany as we know it today did not exist. His experience in the French Army and love for the American view of liberty made him a great choice to serve as an officer in the Continental Army. (nypl)

Brig. Gen. Edward Stevens, approximately 700 strong. Though they were on their way, they were slow moving and their competence as fighting men was unknown.

The biggest challenge Gates had when he arrived was the feeding and supplying of the army. Though he wanted all the forces to concentrate, their dispersed fashion was a blessing in disguise at it allowed them to spread out for provisions. Gates continued to call on the governors of Virginia and North Carolina to send supplies. The forces along Deep River were in desperate shape, and de Kalb clearly laid out the condition of his brigade to Gates. De Kalb had experience as a quartermaster and knew the challenges facing the small army. He explained his intimate feelings of his situation to his wife, "Here I am at last, considerably south, suffering from intolerable heat, the worst of quarters, and the most voracious of insects of every hue and form."

Another pressing issue for Gates was time. Gates received a letter from Thomas Sumter that British forces were concentrating in and around Camden but were still small in number. Sumter urged action, as did Richard Caswell commanding the North Carolina militia. Gates believed unless they acted fast, the Virginia and North Carolina militia would disperse, and the lack of action would discourage Patriots in the Carolinas. Soon after arriving in camp, Gates issued orders that most of his officers could not believe. His men were to "hold themselves in readiness to march at a moment's warning." Colonel Otho Williams, serving as deputy adjutant general, wrote that the officers were "astonished" by the orders. How could an army that could barely eat and low on all necessary supplies take up an active campaign southward? Yet, this was exactly what Gates intended to do: march southwest into South Carolina.

On July 26, Gates issued orders for his army to march with de Kalb in the lead and South Carolinian Lt. Col. Francis Marion and his twenty men riding with Gates personally. The route was a direct route south, via a barren, sandy plain, sparsely inhabited area of South Carolina. Any foodstuffs in the region were already raided by militia. The officers under Gates implored him to take a more circuitous route via Salisbury and Charlotte. This route, though fifty miles longer, provided a more pro Patriot population, more fertile landscape, and safer route for supplies to travel or possibly a retreat in case of a defeat.

The Maryland regiments that de Kalb commanded were some of the finest in the Continental Army. These men fought bravely in the campaign around the city of New York and continued to be called on by Washington to provide stability to his nascent army. The fact that Washington sent these men south speaks to the concern he had for the British threat in the Carolinas. (nypl)

Gates believed a more direct route was necessary for two main reasons: time and reinforcements. First, he believed that it was crucial that his army make a presence in South Carolina as soon as possible to boost morale and encourage the Patriot militias. Second, the North Carolina militia under Caswell still refused to join Gates and was instead moving southward toward South Carolina down the Yadkin and Pee Dee rivers. If this force was overwhelmed by the British, Gates would not just lose a third of his army, but also the morale of North Carolina. Also, Gates believed, through various reports, that the British force in Camden was smaller than his. If he could strike it before it was reinforced, he might gain a quick and decisive victory.

Now it was up to Gates to turn around the American cause in the south. Not everyone was confident of Gates's chances. His officers were not confident in his plan. They believed the army was in no condition for such a march, via the route chosen by Gates, to take on the British. Charles Lee spoke with Gates before the new Southern Department Army commander headed south, and warned him to take care, lest "his northern laurels would be turned into southern willows."

"Before Any Thing of Consequence"

Cornwallis's Dilemma

CHAPTER THREE

When Clinton sailed for New York on June 8, he left Cornwallis approximately 2,500 men under arms. This included British Regulars and Provincial forces. Of course, the intent was to use this as a stable core to build around with newly raised Loyalist regiments and militia. The British army was a volunteer force. Most men who volunteered were farmers, mechanics, and tradesmen who needed steady income. Most of the men in the ranks were in their 20s and, before the American Revolution, had little active military or battle experience. The officers tended to be from a higher social class and had more experience. Great Britain did rely on hired soldiers from the Germany states (popularly called Hessians), and Cornwallis had two Hessian units with him in the Charleston garrison.

Cornwallis called upon three capable officers to assist him in the coming summer months. These men were well known to Cornwallis and served under him throughout the war. Lieutenant Colonel Lord Rawdon was Cornwallis's most reliable officer. An Irish native, he had served in the British army in American conflicts since the battle of Bunker Hill. Rawdon rose in rank and responsibility throughout the war and Cornwallis put him in command of the important post at Camden. Rawdon's command included mostly Provincial troops and Loyalist militia. Though Rawdon was a close friend of Clinton before having a falling out with the senior commander as

Thomas Sumter is buried with his family at the Thomas Sumter Memorial Park near Stateburg, South Carolina. The land was once part of his Home House Plantation. Following the war, Sumter served in Congress and the U.S. Senate. He passed away in 1832 at 97 years old. Many communities and institutions are named after Thomas Sumter, including the University of South Carolina's mascot, the "Gamecocks."
(nypl)

Lord Francis Rawdon was born in Ireland and by age 17 was serving in the British Army as an ensign. In 1773, he was named lieutenant in the 5th Regiment of Foot and was part of the British force sent to Boston in 1774. He served in all the major battles in New England and rose to Colonel of the Volunteers of Ireland. By 1780, he was part of the British Army in South Carolina and had become a respected officer. (ro)

most his officers appeared to do, Cornwallis relied on him heavily.

The next capable officer in Cornwallis's army was Lieut. Col. Banastre Tarleton. One of the more famous officers in the American Revolution, Tarleton by this point had a reputation as being a fierce, aggressive, and ruthless leader. He commanded a legion raised in the Americas and his men were dedicated to their commander. Tarleton had served in the war since 1776, mostly under Cornwallis. Tarleton was one of the most feared British officers in the south.

Finally, Lieut. Col. James Webster was a reliable officer that commanded Cornwallis's old regiment, the 33rd Regiment of Foot. Webster had served in the war since 1775, mostly under Cornwallis. In the summer of 1780, Webster commanded a brigade of British Regulars.

After Clinton's departure, Cornwallis worked hard to not only establish military control but also civilian/political control of South Carolina. He visited Camden, the largest outpost outside of Charleston, to personally meet with his subordinates and discuss their plans moving forward. It was not long after Clinton left Charleston that Cornwallis became faced with one of the biggest challenges of his career: winning over the hearts and minds of the people of South Carolina for the Crown.

Though de Kalb represented the only organized Continental force in the Carolinas, things were not totally quiet. The American surrender at Charleston was a serious blow to the Patriot cause, although American partisans remained active and increased their attacks and raids. Clinton's proclamations, combined with Patriot propaganda, had swelled the ranks of the Patriot partisan units under Thomas Sumter and others like Col. Andrew Williamson. Conversely, the British occupation of South Carolina emboldened Loyalists; thus what erupted across South Carolina was a civil war of Americans on different sides of the "revolution."

Though not official, American partisan leaders divided up South Carolina into west, central, and east districts (reflecting mostly the South Carolina militia division of the state). In the west, the most rural of the state, Andrew Pickens commanded a small contingent of South Carolina militia. Pickens, born in Pennsylvania, had lived in Virginia for a short period before his family migrated south along the Great

(LEFT) Andrew Pickens, born in Pennsylvania, moved to the Waxhaws area of South Carolina as a teenager. He soon became active in the local militia and spent time fighting with the Cherokee on the frontier. As the war broke out, Pickens became a militia captain and was at early fights at Ninety Six and Williamson's Fort. He was captured at Charleston in 1780 and was serving out parole during the Camden campaign. Later that year he would become active again in the South Carolina militia. (nypl)

(RIGHT) Thomas Sumter was originally born in Virginia and served in the Virginia militia fighting Indians on the frontier. By the 1760s, Sumter was living in South Carolina and joined the local militia. In 1776, he joined the 2nd South Carolina as lieutenant colonel and in 1780 served as a brigadier general leading South Carolina partisan units. He was a constant pain in the side of Cornwallis and Tarleton and earned the nickname of "Gamecock." (nypl)

Wagon Road to Waxhaws, South Carolina. Raised as a devout Presbyterian, he fought in the colonial militia in various actions against the Cherokee, and when the American Revolution started, he was appointed a captain in the South Carolina militia. Pickens was active in Georgia as well and his victories there kept most of the Loyalist population from joining the British. He and his militia surrendered to the British and went on parole when Charleston fell, but rejoined the Patriot cause later that year due to what he believed were British breaches of his parole.

Covering the central portion of South Carolina was Thomas Sumter. Sumter, born and raised in Virginia, served in the Virginia militia. He fought in the French and Indian War and was present at Braddock's defeat in 1755. Before the war, Sumter settled near Stateburg, South Carolina and became involved in local affairs. When the American Revolution broke out, Sumter volunteered his services to the Patriot cause and served as a lieutenant colonel, then colonel, in the state militia. By 1780, Sumter became very active along the Wateree River against Loyalist forces. His fierceness in battle earned him the nickname "The Fighting Gamecock" and led to the British burning down his home. Cornwallis and Tarleton both mentioned Sumter's tactics as having a big influence on their campaign in 1780.

Finally, the most famous Patriot partisan was Francis Marion, or the "Swamp Fox." Marion spent most of his time leading his partisans in the eastern portion of the state, using the rivers and swamps to his advantage. Marion was born in South Carolina in Berkeley County and had served in the French and Indian War, becoming a trusted friend of William Moultrie. By the time of the American Revolution, Marion became a captain in the 2nd South Carolina Regiment and fought along with Moultrie at Sullivan's

In 1775, Francis Marion joined the 2nd South Carolina under William Moultrie and fought at Sullivan's Island in the 1776 British attack on Charleston. He was lucky not to be in Charleston when it fell to the British in 1780 because he was recuperating at home from an injury. Afterwards, inspired by what he believed were British atrocities, he formed his own partisan unit and his famed tactics earned him the name "Swamp Fox." (nypl)

Island in June 1776 as well as in the failed attack on Savannah, Georgia, in 1779. In a twist of fate, Marion was not with the American army in Charleston when it fell in May 1780. He was at home recovering from a broken ankle (legend says from jumping out a window to avoid a social obligation at a party in Charleston) and thus missed the surrender of Charleston. When de Kalb arrived in North Carolina with his Maryland and Delaware Continentals, Marion rode with a small contingent of men to meet with him. Marion and the Bavarian hit it off well, and soon de Kalb ordered Marion south to gather intelligence and supplies.

With these three talented partisan leaders operating in South Carolina, Cornwallis and the British army had their hands full. Their goal was not to just control South Carolina, but also raise large provincial units from the Loyalist population. But that proved a hard task as it became near impossible for Cornwallis to protect any Loyalist force that formed that summer.

After the battle of Waxhaws, the Patriot propaganda pushed the narrative of "Buford's Massacre" along with the brutality that Tarleton's men showed the Virginians. This rallying call was effective in polarizing and bringing out Patriot militia and partisan forces. Organized Patriot militia began seeking out opportunities to defeat Loyalist units and outposts. This turned into an all-out civil war in the Carolinas and often turned brutal and ruthless. An example of this fratricide was at Ramsour's Mill, North Carolina on June 20, 1780. Just north of the South Carolina border, Ramsour's Mill became a rallying point for local Loyalists under John Moore. Moore, a veteran of the British victory at Charleston, returned home with Cornwallis's direction to raise a Loyalist militia force but not to assemble until Cornwallis marched into North Carolina, where they could rise with support. By June (and against orders), nearly 1,300 men answered Moore's call, many of whom were new recruits and not armed. Patriot forces in nearby Charlotte heard about Moore's force and decided to act quickly. On the morning of June 20, Patriots attacked Moore's force, first with cavalry then infantry. After briefly being stymied, the Patriot militia forces were able to outflank the Loyalist militia's position and inflict heavy casualties. The fighting, often hand to hand, included a case of a brother killing his own brother. The Patriots, though only

The battle of Ramsour's Mill, fought on June 10, 1780, epitomized the war in the south as a civil war. Here, no regular forces were engaged but Patriot and Loyalist militia units. Families were split with members fighting each other on either side. The Patriot victory was one of many small set backs the British suffered with large implications. Today the battlefield is located behind Lincolnton (NC) High School where a monument is now located. (ro)

numbering 400, completely defeated and dispersed the larger Loyalist force.

The action at Ramsour's Mill was followed up a few weeks later at Williamson's Plantation on July 12. Capt. Christian Huck was encamped with a mixed force of Provincials and Loyalist militia. Huck's mission was to suppress Patriot activity near the North Carolina border and enforce the loyalty oath to the local population. Huck, a Loyalist himself from Philadelphia, had joined the British army in 1778 and recently served under Banastre Tarleton. He was widely hated by the Patriots and was known for his harsh tactics of intimidation and recently burning Hill's Iron Works. Huck, who recently captured local Patriot leaders and was holding them for execution, was looking for local Patriot militia leader Col. William Bratton. After riding to Bratton's home and threatening his wife, Huck's men camped at the nearby home of James Williamson. Word got to Bratton of Huck's atrocities and his location. He moved to attack the Loyalist force early on the morning of July 12.

With his men unaware of the danger, Huck's force was surprised and soon surrounded. Responding to the attack, Huck hurriedly mounted his horse to rally his men. Soon he received a mortal wound to his head, and his men fled or surrendered. Only 24 of his men survived. Though a small battle, the defeat proved that even though the British controlled South Carolina, they could not protect Loyalists from Patriot forces. This hindered Cornwallis's ability to recruit more men to arms and convince civil authorities that the Crown was again in control.

With the demise of Huck, Patriot militia units were energized. Partisan Thomas Sumter began to raise a large force of militia with his sights on British outposts in central South Carolina around the British base camp at Camden. A challenge for Sumter and other militia leaders was to keep the militia in the field and active, or they would return home. Sumter sought British outposts that were lightly defended or isolated, and he turned his sights to a small British fort along the Catawba River called Rocky Mount.

At Rocky Mount, Lieut. Col. George Turnbull of the New York Volunteers commanded nearly 300 men. The impromptu fort included abatis, two log houses, and a clapboard house. On August 1, Sumter's force of 500 militia attacked and dispersed the small camp

Today, the battle of Huck's Defeat is interpreted at historic Brattonsville near Rock Hill, South Carolina and includes several structures that relate to the Bratton Family. A trail leads to the area of the battle. The site is administered by the Culture and Heritage Museums in York County. (sj)

outside of the fort, but all of Turnbull's men retreated into the fort and hunkered down. Sumter ordered two assaults against the fort and then demanded that Turnbull surrender, to which he responded, "Duty and inclination induce me to defend this place to the last extremity." Sumter devised a plan to light the fort on fire by throwing firebrands (pieces of fat lighter/fatwood) onto the fort. Small fires broke out but soon a thunderstorm struck, and heavy rain doused the threatening fires. Demoralized by being stymied for eight hours, Sumter called off his attack. The enthusiasm amongst his men began to diminish, and Sumter knew to cut his losses and live to fight again another day. Sumter suffered 12 total casualties while Turnbull lost 20 as a result of the affair. Sumter, not one to take defeat easily, looked south to a British camp at Hanging Rock.

Just twenty-five miles north of Camden, Hanging Rock was an important British camp established to help protect the British supply depot at Camden. Along with Rocky Mount, Cheraw, and others, these camps and posts were established to help warn the British of any movement from the north toward Camden. These outposts were also to help recruit Loyalists and protect Loyalist families and settlements. In command at Hanging Rock was Irish born Maj. John Carden, commanding a mixed group of Loyalists and British Provincials. Carden, who was recently promoted to command, had his army of 500-1,400 along the road to Camden near Hanging Rock Creek. Carden knew Sumter and other partisans were in the area from regular raids on his men and at Rocky Mount a few days before. His force included the British Legion Infantry, Prince of Wales American Regiment (American raised/Provincial), Loyalist militia, and a handful of dragoons from the British Legion.

On the morning of August 6, Sumter ordered a three-pronged attack at the northern most camp of Loyalists. This quick assault forced the Loyalists to flee south toward the next camp, that of British Legion Infantry and North Carolina militia. The British Legion Infantry stopped Sumter's initial assault, and attempted two bayonet charges, but were driven back and out of action. As they retreated, and Sumter attempted to reform his troops, they were struck by the Prince of Wales Regiment that had moved onto Sumter's right flank. But Sumter's riflemen took to cover behind trees, and soon inflicted heavy casualties on the Prince of Wales Regiment.

Sumter's men pushed southward, though some stopped in the camps to loot for supplies and alcohol. The last British camp was that of the Prince of Wales American Regiment. These men, along with members of the British Legion, were able to stop Sumter's assault and push them back. The battle lasted about three hours, after which Sumter pulled his men off the battlefield.

Carden lost over 270 men with Sumter losing an estimated 60 men. Though Sumter was not able to take the British post at Hanging Rock, he was able to inflict heavy casualties on the British and proved that the Patriot partisans and militia could take on these British outposts. This had a big impact on the effectiveness of Cornwallis's ability to recruit more Loyalists to join his army. The fact that the Patriots were still very active and a threat in South Carolina tampered the Loyalists' enthusiasm.

Though not on the actual battlefield, the Daughters of the American Revolution placed their battle monument at the actual Hanging Rock. (ro)

Sumter kept Gates aware of his movements and actions. Gates was not entirely sure how to use these partisans effectively. Sumter held much disdain for Continental officers as he believed they looked down on him and their militias. Sumter advised Gates to hold the Catawba and Wateree Rivers as a line, with Marion taking the Williamsburg (SC) militia and holding the Santee River. This would keep the British main force toward the east. Gates was not convinced and developed his own plans to move south to Camden; where he pondered on how to use Sumter to his advantage. But he was fully aware that emboldened militia must be kept busy in the field, or they would dissolve as there was no financial or logistical system to support them. This fact was not lost on Lt. Col. Banastre Tarleton when he wrote "minds of men are influenced by enterprize, and that to keep undisciplined people together, it is necessary to employ them."

On August 10, Cornwallis wrote Clinton that Gates was now moving south from his camp near Cox's Mill in North Carolina and was already in South Carolina. Cornwallis, itching to leave administrative duties behind and be in the field, made plans to ride to Camden. He ordered Tarleton to Camden as well as the light infantry from Ninety Six. Cornwallis knew that in order to hold South Carolina and to carry out his plans to move north to North Carolina, he needed to hold Camden. Camden was the key to the backcountry, which was key to the entire state of South Carolina. Additionally, if he could defeat or annihilate the new American army under Gates (a hero due to his victory at Saratoga), maybe the enthusiasm of the revolution in the south would fall. Defeating another major American army in the south should finally drain the life blood out of the partisan units working against him and his plan to raise Loyalist militia units. Either way, he was heading west to Camden and there he would take command in the field, where Cornwallis preferred to be. He wrote to British Vice Admiral Arbuthnot "I hope to get up before any thing of consequence happens."

SOUTH CAROLINA

OLD ST. DAVID'S

St. David's, authorized by the General Assembly in 1768, was the last parish established in colonial S. C. Said to be buried in its churchyard are soldiers of British forces occupying the Cheraws in 1780. The steeple an vestibule of this Episcopal church were added c. 1827 and services held here until a new church was built in 1916.

"Fatigued, and Almost Famished"

Gates Moves Through the Carolinas

CHAPTER FOUR

Camden, South Carolina, in the eighteenth century was a small village and trading post in the South Carolina backcountry along the Wateree River. The town traces its origins to the settlement of "Fredericksburg," that was founded south of the current town. That town did not develop due to its location in a low-lying area, so many settlers settled north of the new village on higher ground. This new settlement was known as "Pine Tree Hill." One of the founders of this new town was Joseph Kershaw, who led the effort to rename this town Camden, after Lord Camden in the British Parliament. Camden became a favorite of the colonists when he supported their opposition to the Stamp Act. The settlement, at the head of navigable waters and along the Great Wagon Road (a road that connected northward to Virginia and beyond) grew steadily and became the civic and cultural center of the region.

By the summer of 1780, Camden was one of the most important crossroads in the American south. After their capture of Charleston, Sir Henry Clinton and Lord Cornwallis made Camden a British military camp and depot. Lord Rawdon commanded Camden and placed detachments north of town in the direction of North Carolina, a known direction of any Continental threat. At Cheraw Hills, he placed Provincial Rangers, the 71st Regiment of Foot (Fraser's Highlanders); Provincials and Loyalist militia were placed at Hanging Rock and Rocky Mount. This

In the spring of 1780, historic Old St. David's and its graveyard were witness to the suffering of the British soldiers who established an outpost along the Pee Dee River in the Cheraw Hills. (ro)

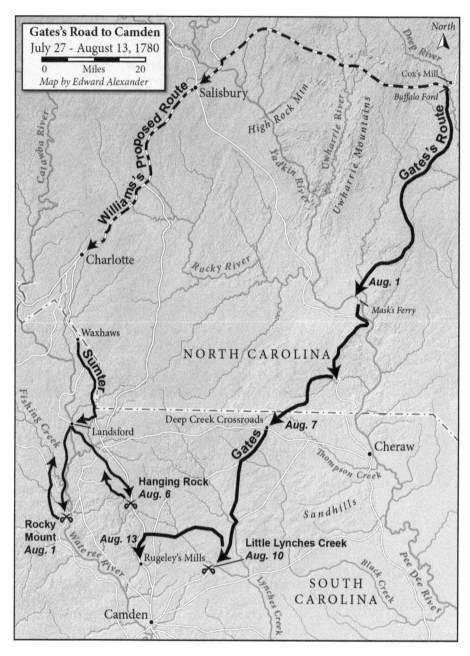

GATES'S ROAD TO CAMDEN—The route Gates chose to Camden was debated at the time and still is today. Gates believed the most direct and fastest route was needed to "save" South Carolina and connect to Caswell's North Carolina militia posted north of Lynches Creek. Otho Williams and others believed an indirect route via Charlotte would support the undersupplied army better.

allowed Rawdon to not only get an early warning if Gates approached, but also allowed him to spread out his units from Camden. The mass of men in the area was turning Camden into an epicenter of disease and sickness in the ranks. These detachments also served to subdue uprisings and protect local Loyalists from Patriot partisans.

The impact of the sickness that hit Cornwallis's army cannot be overstated. The 71st Regiment of Foot suffered severely at Cheraw. The two battalions camped there along the Great Pee Dee River numbered around 300 men. Camped near the river in wet conditions in small huts and tents, the men were overcome with "fevers" (most likely malaria). When the 71st left Cheraw, nearly 40 men were left behind due to their weakened condition. In Camden, Rawdon's men also suffered, putting a strain on the local populace and supplies. Many of the men were "very sickly" and were not capable of a campaign or battle. An estimated 800 men were too ill for duty. Rawdon, and then Cornwallis, knew this well and believed that their small command of around 2,300 men would not hold up well if Gates's army (Rawdon estimated Gates had 5,000 men) attacked them at Camden.

During the summer of 1780, the 71st Regiment of Foot was encamped along the Pee Dee River near St. David's Church. Succumbing to heat, humidity, and spreading disease in the wet area along the river, many men became sick. The church was used as a makeshift hospital and many of the men died there. They were buried in various places outside the church, some are marked today. (ro)

The 71st Regiment of Foot, or "Fraser's Highlanders," were raised in Inverness, Stirling, and Glasgow in 1775 for service in North America. The regiment performed admirably in the New York-New Jersey Campaign and the Philadelphia Campaign. By 1778, they successfully captured Savannah and later defended the city. This memorial stone was placed in 2011 at the supposed site of an officer of the 71st who died in the summer of 1780 along the Pee Dee River. (ro)

The land that Gates led his army over was barren and sandy. This area was the coastal area for a prehistoric ocean; many roads were little more than sandy trails through pine forests with little found to eat. (ro)

Though small in numbers, Cornwallis's army in Camden consisted of some of the best units in the British army. It was a mixed force of Regulars and well-trained provincial troops. Lord Rawdon commanded his own Volunteers of Ireland regiment that consisted of European born Americans (mostly Irish immigrants). They were well trained and very reliable. Rawdon also commanded the British Legion Infantry, Royal North Carolina Regiment, and mixed group of North Carolina Volunteers (Loyalists) militia who arrived in early August, fleeing Gates's army. The 23rd Regiment of Foot (Royal Welch Fusiliers) was formed in the late seventeenth century and served well in the war from the first battle at Lexington. Lieutenant Colonel James Webster's own 33rd Regiment of Foot was considered one of the best trained and disciplined units in the army. Like the 23rd, they were a battle-hardened unit that saw service in Charleston in 1776 and throughout the northern campaigns with Cornwallis. Four companies of the 16th Regiment of Foot along with the light infantry of the 71st Regiment served as light infantry under Webster.

Operating directly under Cornwallis in reserve was Colonel Tarleton's famed British Legion. Formed the year before in Philadelphia of Loyalists from New York, Pennsylvania, and New Jersey, Tarleton's Legion was a mix of foot soldiers and horse soldiers. Of all the British units, Tarleton's Legion is still the most known today. Tarleton was known as a hard riding, ruthless, and aggressive commander. He was hated by Whigs in the south and his ruthless tactics were used by the Continentals to recruit and as propaganda against the British. With all that said, Tarleton's men were effective and feared, two traits that played an important role in the upcoming battle with Gates. The army in Camden also supported artillery, having nine pieces mixed of two, three, and six pounders.

While Lord Rawdon awaited Cornwallis and reinforcements, Gates moved southward. Thomas Pinckney, Gates's newly appointed aide, wrote that Gates believed "we may then as well move forward and starve, as starve lying here." In terms of reinforcements, Gates knew Virginia militia sent to him by Governor Thomas Jefferson was on the way, a few days' march behind. Ahead of him was a large contingent of North Carolina militia commanded by the former North Carolina Governor, Richard Caswell. Gates feared Caswell's advanced position on the Yadkin River put his inexperienced men in danger from Rawdon's forces. Caswell so far was uncooperative in working with de Kalb and then Gates. For success, Gates needed the cooperation of Caswell and hoped there were provisions there as well.

One arm of service that Gates would do without was cavalry. Colonel Anthony White commanded the dragoons of the Southern Army, but this force, once 500 men before the fall of Charleston, was now a shadow of itself. White's men, encamped in and around Halifax, North Carolina, were in no shape to move out on campaign. Gates ordered White to join the army once his men were equipped and ready for campaign. White, along with Lieutenant Colonel William Washington, spent most of the summer in Virginia trying to recruit and refit the dragoons. Gates moved south with just about 60 men under the command of French born Lt. Col. Charles Armand, who commanded the remnants of Count Pulaski's command, and a few partisan fighters under Francis Marion. Unfortunately, one group of people Gates had too many of were women and children. Gates ordered all the women, children, and extra baggage off to Charlotte, but many remained behind.

William Washington was born in Stafford County, Virginia, and was a distant cousin of George Washington. He commanded a company in the famed 3rd VA before he was transferred to several different light dragoon units. Eventually ending up in South Carolina, Washington's dragoons suffered defeats at the battle of Monck's Corner and Lenud's Ferry in the spring of 1780. Afterwards Washington headed back to Virginia to find new recruits and mounts for a reconstituted cavalry force for the southern army. (nypl)

In 1749, Otho Holland Williams was born in Prince George's County, Maryland. Before the war, Williams served an apprenticeship as a clerk but in the spring of 1775 joined a rifle unit. He served in many roles throughout the war and was a well-respected officer. After the war, Williams served in the civil service in various roles in Baltimore. He moved to modern day Williamsport (named in his honor) to lay out the new town. His health began to decline soon after, and he died in 1794 at the age of 46. (nypl)

One of Gates's biggest challenges was crossing the Pee Dee River. This was the largest river crossing Gates faced in his movement south. As soon as his army arrived on August 1, flooding from recent storms and winds delayed the crossing. It took a few days for Gates to get his men across the Pee Dee. On August 4, Gates issued a proclamation to encourage the residents of the Carolinas that he was there to defend them, called for Loyalists to cease their support of the British army, encouraged men to arms, and "to vindicate the rights of America in this state." Gates was not one to shy away from theatrics.

Gates pushed a positive narrative, but his men and officers saw a different picture. Colonel Otho Williams wrote that the men in the ranks were "Fatigued, and almost famished, their patience began to forsake them, their looks began to be vindictive, mutiny was ready to manifest itself." As predicted, the land was barren, and the heat wore on the men. The land provided little sustenance for the army. As Otho Williams wrote, many homes were "abandoned by the owners and plundered by the neighbors." The men had little foodstuffs, and had to rely on unripe fruit, corn, and a ration of less than half a pound of beef. Williams famously noted that officers thickened their soup with their wig powder. Gates wrote a flurry of letters to various governors calling on them for assistance. He wrote to North Carolina Governor Abner Nash about the "deplorable state of the Commissary and Quarter Masters Departments, and the entire Deficiency of Magazines, to Supply the Southern Army." Gates was still under the impression that Lord Rawdon's forces in and around Camden were much reduced. He also believed correctly that Cornwallis was in Charleston and had little concern that Cornwallis might soon lead the forces at Camden. Though the "Gamecock" Thomas Sumter provided great partisan service, his intelligence gathering was subpar and missed Cornwallis's movement to Camden, which impacted Gates's decisions.

The weakened condition of his men did not slow Gates down. He received word on August 5 from Caswell that he had plans to attack Lord Rawdon's forces along Little Lynches Creek. Gates feared a disaster and pushed on to join the North Carolina militia. Finally, on August 7, Caswell and his 2,000 North Carolina militiamen joined Gates's army at Deep Creek Crossroads. To many, this large

contingent was the main reason Gates took this route south, but when they joined the North Carolinians, it was obvious the militia were not ready for a hard campaign nor suited for military life. Gates was beyond frustrated with Caswell; not only had Caswell not responded to many of Gates's letters, but his men also had "gleaned the Country." The relationship with the former North Carolina governor, now militia general was strained at best. With his army now doubled in size, Gates reorganized his force and prepared for a coming battle.

By August 9, the lead elements of Gates's reorganized army under Col. Charles Porterfield made contact with Rawdon's forces along Little Lynches Creek. Porterfield commanded light infantry and the small cavalry force under Lt. Col. Armand. It was clear to Porterfield that Rawdon was in a strong position along Little Lynches Creek. Rawdon knew Gates was approaching and had called in some of his posts and consolidated his force along a natural defensible barrier. Gates quickly moved his army to join Porterfield and issued orders for August 10 for "the whole army . . . to be held in Readiness to parade at the Shortest Notice . . . The General hopes to find his Officers and Men alert, and always prepared for Action."

One important geographic hurdle for Gates's army's southward movement was the Pee Dee River. Gates's army crossed the river at Mask's (or Mast's) Ferry. Due to the logistics of crossing this large river and weather, it took several days for the army to cross. Today, the original road and ferry location are on private property. (ro)

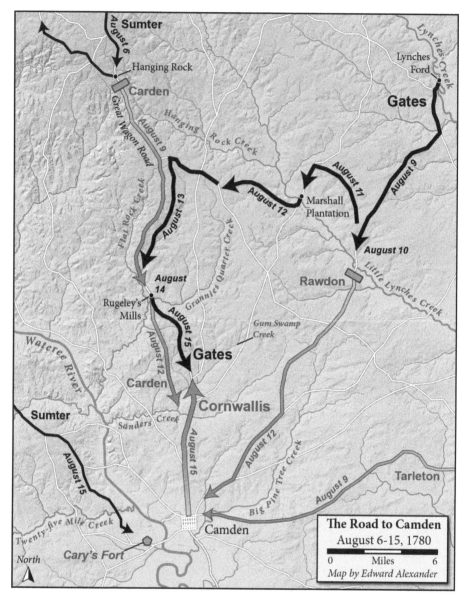

THE ROAD TO CAMDEN—Dealing with geographic and military obstacles, Gates had to shift from his direct route to Camden westward to Rugeley's Mills on the Old Wagon Road. Some of Gates's route is documented by primary sources, but some of the route remains conjecture based on historic roads and fords.

On August 10, the much-anticipated encounter between Gates and the British in South Carolina took place along the banks of Little Lynches Creek. Rawdon, after sitting in Camden, decided that he needed to slow down Gates's push forward to allow for more reinforcements to reach Camden. The best natural barrier for this was Lynches Creek and Little Lynches Creek. These two tributaries of the Pee Dee River cut across Gates's route to Camden. Rawdon originally posted along Lynches Creek but decided to pull back to a higher position on the south bank of Little Lynches Creek. Here Rawdon put his infantry near one of the few bridges across the creek. The creek was not wide but had steep banks, a marshy bottom area, and was heavily wooded, hiding both armies from clear view of each other. Rawdon knew at this point he was outnumbered by Gates, but believed the geography would favor him and slow his approach.

The original Kershaw House was burned during the Civil War by Union soldiers. Today, the house has been rebuilt as part of the Historic Camden site. The British used Joseph Kershaw's home as their headquarters while he was exiled to the Caribbean. He returned after the war to help rebuild the ruined town. (ro)

Armand's Legion, probing the British position, came under fire from British sentries around the bridge. Soon, more Patriot riflemen joined in the long fire fight across the creek with no one suffering any noted casualties other than one of Armand's men captured by the British. Though Rawdon thought about ordering an attack through a gap in the swamp that went undetected by Gates, he ultimately decided against it as his major objective was to delay Gates as long as possible. Rawdon attempted to lure Gates into attacking him by moving further away from the banks, but Gates determined a frontal assault was not practical with his inexperienced army against an enemy on advantageous ground. Finally, on August 12, Gates decided to move his army north to a crossing of Little Lynches Creek that was around Rawdon's flank. Gates ordered the march for 8 a.m., to be accomplished with "as little noise as possible." Gates's objective was Rugeley's Mills, north of Camden. Rawdon had tied up Gates for two days and added dozens of miles to Gates's march to Camden by forcing him to go the roundabout route via Rugeley's Mills.

With Gates's move north around Rawdon's flank, Rawdon determined to fall back and consolidate his remaining forces at Camden. Rawdon later received a few companies of light infantry from Ninety Six, and then the arrival of Lord Cornwallis on August 13. Rawdon called on all able-bodied men in Camden to join him in defense of the post. The call was not overly successful as Rawdon recorded imprisoning 160 men in the local jail. Cornwallis took time to inspect the garrison and troops at Camden and came to the same realization that Rawdon had before: if the British were going to hold Camden they had to move out and attack Gates's army. He did not believe he could abandon the town, however, as too many of the

Colonel Charles Armand Tuffin was a lesser known French officer who came to America to support the war for independence. His ship was attacked on its way to America, and he was one of only three who were able to swim to the coast and survive. He took command of the Pulaski Legion after the death of Pulaski—his forces in the Camden campaign were much deteriorated, undermanned and supplied. (nypl)

men in the hospitals could not be moved, nor could the stores of provisions. Once he could prepare his men to move, he would go on the offensive and search out Gates's army.

After moving around Rawdon, Gates moved his men west to Rugeley's Mills on the Great Wagon Road on August 13. The area, also known as Clermont, was about thirteen miles north of Camden. Located along the Great Wagon Road at Grannies Quarter Creek, the area was owned by local Loyalist Col. Henry Rugeley. At Clermont, Rugeley built a large commercial and industrial complex complete with a grist and saw mill, tanyard, stores and warehouses. Rugeley was a Royal merchant who hoped to make a decent profit off of the British occupation of South Carolina via his complex at Clermont and associated store in Charleston. On August 14, the Virginia militia, 700 strong, arrived under Brig. Gen. Edward Stevens. They were a welcome addition to Gates's army on paper, but many were untried and little trained. Their inexperience in marching in the heat forced them to mostly march overnight. They had just endured a similar march, with little provisions, that Gates's men had experienced. But these men were not trained soldiers and were in little shape for action. Many worried that these men could not be relied upon in a coming battle. One Virginian wrote "We were marched almost Night and Day and kept a half allowance of Flour for Eight or Ten days before the Battle. That from these Circumstances and being wholly unacquainted with Military Discipline."

On August 15, Gates began to finalize his plans to move against Camden. In the morning he ordered Francis Marion and his men to the southeast. Gates wanted Marion to take command of the Williamsburg militia, watch the British movements, and destroy boats in the Santee River that a defeated Cornwallis might need to retreat from Camden to Charleston. A few days earlier on August 13, Gates, under the encouragement of Thomas Sumter, decided to send 100 Maryland Continentals and 300 North Carolina militiamen (as well as two brass three pounders) to join Sumter and move down the western side of the Wateree. From this location Sumter could attack supplies and reinforcements going into Camden from Ninety Six to the west. Gates's confidence was evident.

As Gates made his final disposition to move south, Sumter's militia along with his Continental detachment met some success west of Camden. The Wateree River flowed south just one mile west of Camden. Near the important Wateree Ferry that served the major route west from Camden, Loyalist Lt. Col. James Cary built a small fort on his farm near the ferry. Sumter was aware of the fort and decided to see if he could capture it. When Col. Thomas Taylor of Sumter's command launched the attack, most of the defenders inside were asleep, and the others were deceived by Patriot militia dressed just like those occupying the fort. The Loyalists immediately surrendered. Sumter reported that his men killed 7 and captured 30 prisoners, including Cary. Also included in the loot were 38 wagons of supplies and nearly 300 head of cattle. After capturing Cary's Fort, Sumter was also able to attack and capture a relief column from Ninety Six to Camden. Sumter's spoils from this attack numbered nearly 70 prisoners and numerous wagons. Sumter also reaffirmed his earlier intelligence to Gates by writing that the British in Camden "do not exceed two thousand, and not as many as one thousand of the militia, who are generally sickly, and much dispirited." Sumter's intelligence, though not accurate, gave Gates encouragement on the upcoming movement toward Camden.

After the battle of Camden, Governor Richard Caswell resigned from service and returned home. A year later, Caswell was again appointed to command North Carolina militia. After the war, he served in the North Carolina General Assembly and passed away in 1789. He is buried outside of Kinston at the Governor Caswell Memorial. (ro)

"An Advantageous Situation"

The Eve of Battle

CHAPTER FIVE

Land in this area was dotted with tall, Long Leaf Pine trees, the tops of which created a canopy overhead that made for little to no undergrowth. As work continues to return the battlefield back to its 1780 appearance, this modern image provides a sense of what the soldiers saw during the battle. (mw)

The sound of the men's feet was muffled as they shuffled along the white sandy road toward Camden. They were getting tired; the night was humid. Visibility was good, though, as the moon was nearly full. Horatio Gates had put his "Grand Army" into motion around 10 p.m. on the night of August 15.

With the recent arrival of Edward Steven's 700 Virginians, and Thomas Sumter's subsequent foray with his militia down the west side of the Wateree to choke off possible British supplies and troops coming east from the post at Ninety Six, Gates had determined that the time had come to redeploy. Believing, as did the British, that Rugeley's Mills was not a secure, defensible position, upon his arrival there on August 13 Gates had almost immediately sought information regarding sites closer to the British garrison, which was now consolidated within the defenses at Camden. That afternoon, he sent his capable engineering officer, the European Lt. Col. John Christian Senf, along with Lt. Col. Charles Porterfield, south along the Great Wagon Road toward Camden to reconnoiter. Returning from the scout, Senf recommended a defensible spot about halfway between Rugeley's Mills and the town. In his later report to Congress regarding the affair, Gates indicated that upon receiving the engineer's report he resolved to ". . . take post in an Advantageous Situation, with a deep creek in front, about seven miles from Camden."

It was thought by some at the time that Gates's intention in moving the army closer to the British was to use what he believed to be his numerical superiority to attack and overwhelm a smaller enemy force. In a communication to his acting deputy adjutant general, the Marylander Lt. Col. Otho Holland Williams, who would later pen a detailed account of the action at Camden, General Gates relayed to him "a rough estimate of the forces under his command, making them upwards of 7,000." British strength was, at the time, estimated to be around 2,500, with several hundred ill and unfit for duty. Based on these troop figures, or what he believed them to be, an argument could reasonably be made that, at least initially, Gates was indeed contemplating a surprise attack on the British on the night of August 15, 1780. According to his aide-de-camp, Maj. Thomas Pinckney of South Carolina, a staunch supporter of the general, this move by Gates was not done with the desire to attack, however, "but for the purpose of occupying a strong position so near him as to confine his operations, to cut off his supplies of provisions, and to harass him." Such a move, therefore, to confine and harass the British is more logical, as it would be reminiscent of the strategy that had worked so well for Gates against British General John Burgoyne at Bemis Heights during the fighting at Saratoga in 1777.

On the afternoon of the 15th, Gates called "all the general officers in the army, to a council, to be held in Rugeley's Barn." Gates presented his plan to march south, with no objections voiced by the officers in attendance. According to the engineer Lt. Col. Senf, "It was unanimously agreed upon to march that night the army to that creek, by which means they could get a more secure encampment, come nearer Genl Sumter, occupy the road on the east side of Wateree River, and would be able to get nearer intelligence of the enemy." Otho Holland Williams later wrote that while there were no dissenting votes by the officers present (according to Gates), there were a few who harbored misgivings on the possible success of an American army comprised of so many green, untested militiamen. Still, the orders were issued; the army would "march at 10 PM at Night."

Upon learning of General Gates's dubious estimate of his army's troop strength, and not mandated to attend the council with the general officers, Lt. Col. Williams had gone about the business of ascertaining

Maj. Thomas Pinckney was a South Carolinian and served as aide-de-camp to General Gates during the battle of Camden. Later, he served as governor of South Carolina and as George Washington's ambassador to Great Britain. (nypl)

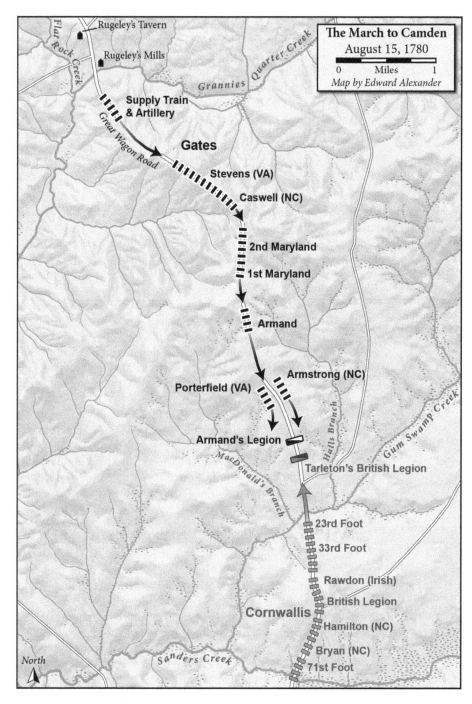

The March to Camden
August 15, 1780

0   Miles   1

Map by Edward Alexander

Rugeley's Tavern

Rugeley's Mills

Flat Rock Creek

Quarter Creek

Grannies

Supply Train & Artillery

Great Wagon Road

Gates

Stevens (VA)

Caswell (NC)

2nd Maryland

1st Maryland

Armand

Armstrong (NC)

Porterfield (VA)

Armand's Legion

MacDonald's Branch

Hall's Branch

Tarleton's British Legion

Gum Swamp Creek

23rd Foot

33rd Foot

Rawdon (Irish)

British Legion

Cornwallis

Hamilton (NC)

Bryan (NC)

71st Foot

North

Sanders Creek

THE MARCH TO CAMDEN—This map details the routes taken by both armies as they made their way toward one another beginning in the late evening of August 15. It also displays the approximate order of march for both sides.

Beginning in Philadelphia, this road wound its way south through Maryland and Virginia into lands being settled in North and South Carolina. It cut through the center of what became the battlefield at Camden. This image was taken in 2022 on the Camden battlefield. (mw)

a more reliable return from the field officers. In a lengthy description by Williams, he "busied himself in collecting these returns and forming an abstract for the general's better information. This abstract was presented to the general just as the council broke up . . . He (Gates) cast his eyes upon the numbers of rank and file present fit for duty, which was exactly three thousand and fifty-two." Horatio Gates has been criticized over the years for not initially having an accurate account of his army's strength. When learning, however, that he commanded an army not of 7,000 troops but rather an army of just over 3,000, placing them more on even terms with the British, the General seemed not to be deterred. He stated to Williams that "these are enough for our purposes." But what exactly were those "purposes"?

Creating a defensive position on the opposite bank above "a deep creek" made good sense. Based on Senf's recommendation, then, it was Gates's apparent intention to march his army south along the Great Wagon Road to the ford at Sanders Creek, where he would prepare a defensive line in hopes of luring the British into an attack. The location was well chosen as it was the only fordable spot along the creek for several miles.

The Patriot army began to prepare for the night's march. According to General Gates, he ordered all heavy and excess baggage north, along with all remaining camp followers, to the safety of the Waxhaws. Ammunition wagons and other necessary baggage would make the march to Camden. The army, tired, hungry, and constantly without adequate supplies, needed to be fed. Before the march, Gates made a momentous decision: he would feed his hungry and depleted troops a full meal out of the hospital stores. This would include a gill (4 ounces) of molasses in place of rum, of which the army had none. Otho Holland Williams wrote: "As there were no spirits yet arrived in camp; and as, until lately, it was unusual for troops to make a forced march, or prepare to meet an enemy without some extraordinary allowance, it was unluckily conceived that molasses, would, for once, be an acceptable substitute." The effect on the men's digestive systems was almost immediate. According to Williams: "The troops of General Gates' army, had frequently felt the bad consequences of eating bad provisions; but, at this time, a hasty meal of quick baked bread and fresh beef, with a desert of molasses, mixed with mush, or dumplings, operated so cathartically, as to disorder very many of the men, who were breaking the ranks all night, and were certainly much debilitated before the action commenced in the morning."

Sergeant William Seymour of the Delaware Line concurred with Williams. "You must observe that instead of rum we had a gill of molasses per man served out to us," Seymour remembered, "which instead of enlivening our spirits, served to purge us as well as if we had taken jallap."

Gates put his weak, exhausted, and ill army on the road to Camden around 10 that night. The vanguard was comprised of troopers from Armand's Legion, commanded by Lt. Col. Charles Armand. On Armand's right, operating as flankers about 200 or so yards through the woods, marched the Virginia Continental light infantry, commanded by Lt. Col. Porterfield. On the left of the road, at a similar distance, was infantry from the North Carolina militia under Maj. John Armstrong. Back in the road itself, Armand's light infantry followed behind his cavalry. Next in line came the 1st and 2nd Maryland Brigades respectively. Marching with the 2nd Maryland Brigade were the men of the 1st Delaware Regiment. Following the Continentals was the North Carolina militia, commanded by General Caswell, and General Stevens's Virginia militia. A rear guard of mounted troops accompanied the supply wagons, with the artillery in the rear. The two Continental brigades were each accompanied by two fieldpieces.

The column slinked its way south along the sandy road for about four and a half hours before it reached a slight rise about a half mile above Gum Swamp Creek. The terrain was rolling and wooded; large trees, Longleaf pines, towered high above, creating a canopy that made for little or no underbrush. North Carolina militiaman Guilford Dudley described the landscape as "open piney wood plains, destitute of brush wood." Luckily for the column, visibility that night was extremely good due to the brightness of the nearly full moon. The white sand of the roadbed stood out keenly to the eye as the road wound its way through the woods. Lieutenant Colonel Armand had disagreed with Gates regarding the placement of his cavalry in the van. He argued that cavalry had never been posted ahead of an infantry column marching at night. The colonel believed that his commander's order was an insult. The feeling was probably justified.

According to Thomas Pinckney, "In Armand's Corps, the General from previous knowledge, had no confidence." But Gates believed that should they meet with trouble, the troopers acting as a screening force would be able to withstand the shock of any attack on their front, while Porterfield's and Armstrong's light infantry units along the flanks could provide additional support.

As it turned out, trouble was closer than anyone thought. At around 2:30 a.m., the Americans were nearing their destination of Sanders Creek which was just two miles beyond. Colonel Armand's vedette, or mounted scout, was several hundred yards ahead of the column, moving down the slope toward shallower Gum Swamp Creek, when a voice came out of the darkness ahead; a challenge. Then all hell broke loose. A pistol shot suddenly rang out, its report echoing through the woods; more shots followed. Men were suddenly yelling. Unaware of each other's presence, the American and British armies had suddenly bumped into one another on the road.

It was arguably the biggest coincidence of the war. As the Patriot army set out toward Camden at 10 at night on the 15th, the British army had likewise moved out along the road from Camden, on their way to attack Gates's army, whom they thought were in camp at Rugeley's Mills. Commanding all British forces in the South, Lt. Gen. Earl Cornwallis had arrived in Camden on August 13, the same day Gates had reached Rugeley's. Cornwallis's plan to subdue the South had been compromised by the presence of the Southern American Army and it was His Lordship's intention to alleviate that problem. American prisoners, taken by Lt. Col. Tarleton's troops, indicated during interrogation that Gates was planning to march to Camden in order to attack the British garrison. Though ultimately there was no truth to this, it was enough to put the British on high alert. Not wishing to leave the country open to the rebels or to abandon his sick troops in Camden, Cornwallis made the decision to strike first. He stated his reasoning in a report to Lord George Germain, the Secretary of State for the Colonies: "However, the greatest part of the troops that I had being perfectly good, and having left Charles Town sufficiently garrisoned and provided for a siege, and seeing so little to lose by a defeat, and much to gain by a victory, I resolved to take the first good opportunity to attack the rebel army."

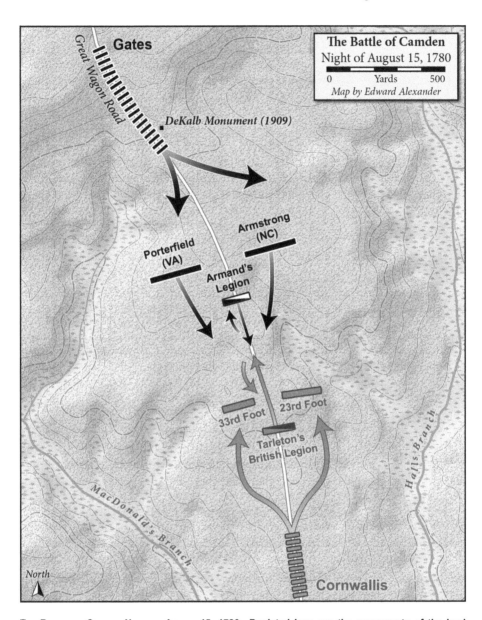

THE BATTLE OF CAMDEN, NIGHT OF AUGUST 15, 1780—Depicted here are the movements of the lead elements of both armies after the initial shock of having their vanguards suddenly encounter one another on the Great Wagon Road around 2:30 a.m.

Moving out at roughly the same time as Gates's army, the British marched north toward Rugeley's Mills. Like the American column, they too were led by cavalry. Under the command of Lt. Col. James Webster, the British van consisted of approximately 20 horsemen from Tarleton's British Legion, known as the

Green Horse, and were followed by a like number of mounted infantry and four companies of light infantry. Behind them marched the Royal Welch Fusiliers, 23rd Regiment of Foot and its sister regiment, Cornwallis's own 33rd Regiment of Foot. Next in succession came Lord Francis Rawdon's Volunteers of Ireland, the British Legion Infantry, Lt. Col. John Hamilton's Royal North Carolina Regiment, the North Carolina Loyalist Militia under Col. Samuel Bryan, and two battalions of the 71st Regiment of Foot, Fraser's Highlanders. Supply wagons and the remainder of Tarleton's cavalry brought up the rear. Six fieldpieces accompanied the British column. Roughly 2,300 strong, the British crossed deep Sanders Creek around midnight. They experienced some confusion during the crossing and needed time to straighten their ranks. By the time the vanguards of the two armies clashed, however, the British column was back in fine order.

Upon the first contact, Armand's vedette, according to Guilford Dudley, "at that instant emptied his pistol, and came clattering in with all the speed his horse could make." More shots were fired as Tarleton's Green Horse immediately charged. They met Armand's surprised cavalry head on in the road with slashing sabers and horse pistols blazing. Quickly recovering from the shock, on the American right, Col. Porterfield's light infantry swept in and opened fire as they had been ordered, stemming the attack of the dragoons. Porterfield would be mortally wounded before ordering his troops to fall back; " . . . a horrid wound in his left leg, a little before the knee, which shattered it to pieces," Guilford Dudley remembered. The British light infantry then took up the attack and forced the Patriots back in the center. Likewise, the British 23rd and 33rd regiments moved up and deployed across the road, opening a brisk fire. Armand's horsemen were quickly pushed back into the light infantry and then further back into the Regulars of the 1st Maryland Brigade. The American column was beginning to collapse upon itself, squeezing together like an accordion. Many of John Armstrong's militiamen on the left flank had fled in the confusion of the first shots but, ultimately, the Patriot infantry had been able to deploy enough to stabilize the line. Both sides now started to pull back. After this initial exchange, the fire from both sides slackened. The fight was short, perhaps only fifteen minutes.

Although the major exchange of fire was over, nerves were tense and there was scattered gunfire throughout the night as both sides hunkered down to wait for daylight. British and Patriot cavalry stayed busy, though, patrolling the woods. Both were able to secure prisoners. Now both commanders would learn just who it was in front of them in the darkness. According to Otho Williams, General Gates was shocked to learn that it was Lord Cornwallis himself who opposed him. "Some prisoners were taken on both sides; from one of these, the deputy adjutant general of the American Army (Williams), extorted information respecting the situation and numbers of the enemy," Williams recalled. The interrogation revealed, " . . . that Lord Cornwallis commanded in person about three thousand regular British troops, which were in line of march, about five or six hundred yards in front. The general's astonishment could not be concealed." After receiving this intelligence, Gates called for another council of war.

"Gentlemen, What Is Best to Be Done?"

Patriot Strategy

CHAPTER SIX

White, acrid smoke from spent gunpowder hung low in the humid air as the men of both armies withdrew, ultimately several hundred yards apart. The American Continentals and militia began to re-form across the Great Wagon Road in the pre-dawn of August 16. Just behind the line, Horatio Gates met again with his general officers.

Having no time for amenities, the General came straight to the point, "Gentlemen," he said, "what is best to be done?" There was a short pause. Finally, General Stevens spoke up, "Gentlemen, is it not too late now to do anything but fight?" This is a question that historians have debated for over two centuries. Were there other options? Could the mixed Patriot units have extricated themselves successfully from the scene, avoiding altogether a confrontation in the open woods with the cream of the British army? Gates's aide, Maj. Thomas Pinckney, for one, believed the answer to that question was no. "It is suggested that the army should have retreated after the skirmish in the night," Pinckney noted, "But a little attention to the detail of the business will render it evident that such an attempt would have been more hazardous than risking the engagement on the ground occupied; and that the opinion of Gen'l Stevens was correct."

The Patriot forces were indeed strung out along the road, stretching back toward Rugeley's Mills. Getting the various regiments turned about in the road and into a line of march would have been

Virginia militiamen under Gen. Edward Stevens were posted in this approximate location on the field to the left of Gen. Richard Caswell's North Carolinians. Most of these militiamen were raw recruits, having received little, if any, battlefield experience. They were pitted on this day against some of the most experienced British Regular troops under the command of Lord Cornwallis, on the east side of the Great Wagon Road. (mw)

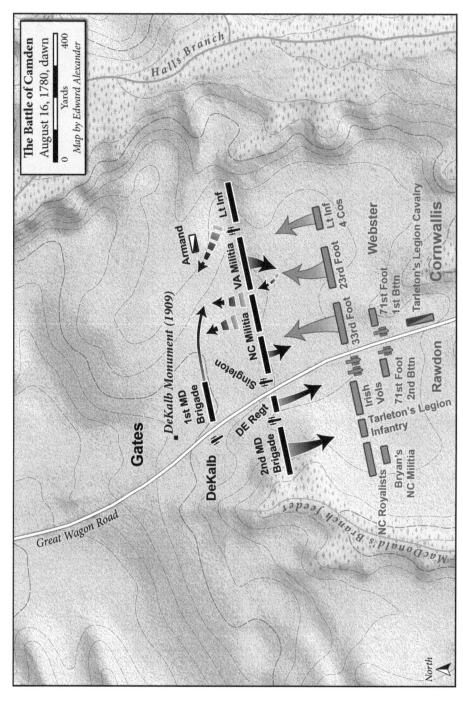

THE BATTLE OF CAMDEN, AUGUST 16, 1780, DAWN—Battle lines and troop placements for both armies at dawn on August 16 are reflected on this map, depicting the opening moments of the battle when the green militiamen from Virginia and North Carolina retreated in panic on the Patriot left flank.

difficult enough, but adding to that difficulty were the ammunition wagons, supply wagons, and artillery that were behind the men as well. With Cornwallis's forces nearby and now on high alert, conducting a silent retreat on a bright, moonlit night would no doubt have been the Devil's own work.

Perhaps though, not all of Gates's officers concurred with his decision to stand and fight. "Well, and has the general given you orders to retreat the army?" Baron de Kalb had asked of Otho Williams when the former was summoned to the council of war. The German-born, 59-year-old de Kalb was a seasoned veteran of many European battlefields, trained in the art of battlefield maneuver. Fighting with the French army during the Seven Years War, he was commended for his expert handling of the army's retreat after its loss at Wilhelmsthal in 1762. Now in South Carolina, after being stopped short of the apparent destination of Sanders Creek in the brief night action, rather than a general retreat, it is logical that de Kalb may have envisioned the Patriot army at least falling back to a more defensible position. Experienced in maneuvering much larger bodies of troops, de Kalb would be well-suited to lead such a redeployment if called upon. If he had misgivings regarding Gates's decision to stand fast with his army holding its current position, however, the Baron apparently did not voice them to his commander. So, the American Patriots would remain, going into line of battle right where they were.

This historical marker on Flat Rock Road just outside the town of Camden commemorates the battle that was fought there on August 16, 1780. (mw)

The formation of his battle line is where Horatio Gates has received the bulk of the criticism that has come his way since that humid August morning. Like his opposite number, Gates would post his veteran troops, the hard-bitten Continentals, on the right, west of the Great Wagon Road. The 2nd Maryland Brigade, consisting of the 2nd, 4th, and 6th Maryland Regiments along with Lt. Col. Joseph Vaughn's venerable Delaware Regiment, was commanded by Brig. Gen. Mordecai Gist and would anchor the American right flank. Along their extreme right was the marshy ground of MacDonald's Branch which, it was believed, would offer a modicum of protection against a flanking movement by the Redcoats.

With Baron de Kalb in overall command of the units west of the road, the Patriot right would be held by some of the toughest combat troops to ever serve in the Continental Army.

Brig. Gen. Mordecai Gist was a member of a prominent family and initially served as a major in the 1st Maryland Regiment. He received promotion to brigadier general and commanded the 2nd Maryland Brigade at the battle of Camden. (nypl)

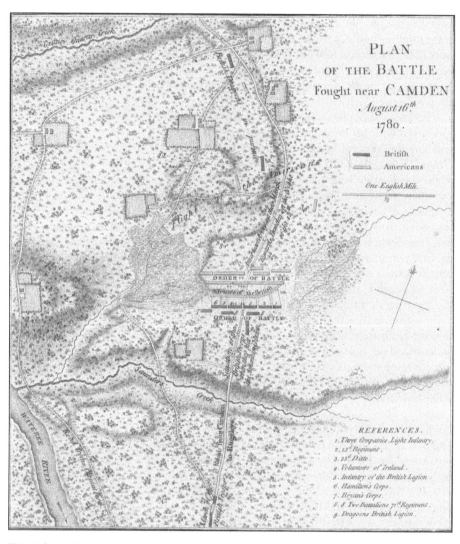

To the left, on the east side of the road in the main battle line, Gates posted his inexperienced militia, beginning with the 1,200 North Carolina militiamen under the command of General Caswell. Standing to their left, on slightly higher ground, were General Stevens's 700 Virginia militiamen. The extreme left flank was protected by approximately 400 of Porterfield's light infantry. Just beyond the flank was a low-lying creek, Halls Branch. In reserve, behind the Virginians, Gates placed around 60 troopers of Armand's cavalry. Also acting in reserve, straddling the road roughly 200 yards behind the main battle line, was the 400 men of Brig. Gen. William Smallwood's crack 1st Maryland Brigade, consisting of the 1st,

This eighteenth century map of the battle was published in London in 1787. (nypl)

3rd, 5th, and 7th Maryland regiments, along with one fieldpiece.

As for the rest of the Patriot artillery, two bronze six-pounders, under the command of Capt. Anthony Singleton, straddled the road in the main line, while two guns each were placed on the right and left flanks.

Several hundred yards in front of the Patriots, down a gentle slope and with Gum Swamp Creek in their rear, Lord Cornwallis had ordered his troops, many of whom were still in column, to lie on their arms and wait for daylight. As dawn neared, Cornwallis delivered his orders for deployment and, like his American counterpart, his Lordship posted his most experienced troops on his right. They would face green Patriot militiamen. On the extreme right flank was posted four companies of light infantry near Halls Branch. To their left were the veteran troops of the 23rd and 33rd Regiments of Foot, respectively. The British right was commanded by Lt. Col. James Webster.

This photograph depicts the fear that a young Patriot militiaman would most likely have felt in the opening minutes of the fight at Camden. The sight of the veterans of the British 23rd and 33rd Regiments of Foot, surging forward in the open woods, ultimately proved more than the green militiamen on the Patriot left were prepared to endure. (mw)

Left of the road, under the command of the capable Lord Rawdon and facing the American Continentals, was the Volunteers of Ireland Regiment. Posted on their left were the infantry companies of Tarleton's British Legion and Lt. Col. John Hamilton's Royal North Carolina Provincials. Behind them, the Volunteer Militia of Col. Samuel Bryan stood in support. Bryan, a Loyalist whose extended family helped settle the Yadkin River Valley in western North Carolina, was a kinsman by marriage of frontiersman Daniel Boone.

Posted behind the main battle line in reserve, from right to left across the road, were the 1st and 2nd Battalions of the 71st Infantry Regiment, respectively. Each battalion boasted a six-pounder fieldpiece. Tarleton's Green Horse formed the remaining portion of the reserve, gathered up just behind the 71st, east of the road.

The rest of Lord Cornwallis's artillery was placed near the road, on the right of the Volunteers of Ireland. There were four fieldpieces here, two six-pounders and two three-pounders.

As dawn approached, Horatio Gates rode along his main battle line, delivering words of encouragement to his troops. In the distance, the sound of the morning gun from Camden was heard. Gates then posted himself behind the reserve troops of the 1st Maryland Brigade.

Captain Singleton, commanding the two 6-pounders in the road, suddenly detected movement from the woods in front of him. British troops were deploying from column, around 200 yards away. He quickly informed the adjutant, Lt. Col. Williams, who wrote: "At dawn of day the enemy appeared in front, advancing in column. Captain Singleton, who commanded some pieces of artillery, observed that he plainly perceived the ground of the British uniform at about two hundred yards in front." Hoping to disrupt the British deployment, Williams immediately ordered Singleton to open fire. He then galloped back to the rear to find General Gates.

While explaining the artillery fire, Williams also informed the General that "the enemy seemed to be displaying their column by the right." According to Williams, there was no response from Gates and he issued no orders. "The general seemed disposed to await events," remembered Williams. Undaunted, Williams then suggested that perhaps the British deployment on their own right could be further disrupted. "The deputy adjutant general observed, that if the enemy, in the act of displaying, were briskly attacked by General Stevens' brigade, which was already in line of battle, the effect might be fortunate." Gates then seemed to come out of his stupor. "Sir, said the General, 'that's right—let it be done.'" Lt. Col. Williams quickly galloped off to deliver the order to General Stevens to attack with his Virginians. Williams later claimed that this was the last order he received from Gates on that day.

Gates then sent his aide, Thomas Pinckney, to inform Baron de Kalb to likewise advance his line of Continentals on the right in tandem with the militia. He also ordered his reserve, Smallwood's 1st Maryland Brigade, to move up, to the left, and occupy the ground now being vacated by the Virginians.

After delivering the order to Stevens to advance, Lt. Col. Williams requested that he be given "forty or fifty privates, volunteers, who would run forward of the brigade and commence the attack." The request was granted and the skirmishers were led forward to within about forty or fifty yards of the enemy. They were ordered to "take to the trees" and keep up a "brisk fire." It was hoped that this tactic would further disrupt the British and cause them to return a scattered fire at once rather than await an order to open with a general volley, which could possibly unnerve the

As colonel of the 1st Maryland Regiment early in the war, William Smallwood served with distinction and was promoted to major general. He commanded the 1st Maryland Brigade at the battle of Camden. (nypl)

raw Patriot militiamen. The skirmishers did as they were instructed, but the effect of their fire against the forming veteran British troops was small.

After taking several casualties on their right from Patriot artillery fire, the remainder of Lord Cornwallis's troops had finished their deployment and prepared their own advance when the Virginians struck. This movement by the militia, however, was misinterpreted by the British as a simple rearrangement of their lines. To Cornwallis, it offered him his own opportunity to strike. "I perceived that the Enemy…were formed in two lines opposite & near to us," he wrote, "and observing a movement on their left, which I supposed to be with an intention to make some alteration in their order, I directed Lt. Colonel Webster to begin the attack." Lord Rawdon, commanding on the left of the road, was given the same instructions.

The pungent smoke from the artillery fire hung eerily in the air, trapped by the canopy of tall pines. It was darker now as the moon was setting before the dawn. Suddenly, from the woods to the south, military drums slammed out; British Regulars were on the move. By all accounts, the Patriot militia began falling back almost immediately, and it was the Virginians who broke first. The sight of the Regulars coming on through the open woods, cheering and shouting, with muskets aslant and bayonets fixed, apparently proved too much for the untested militiamen. Stevens reminded his troops of their own bayonets, which were issued to them only the day before, but to no avail; the panic had already begun. It was too late. All at once the Virginians were on the run, most of them throwing away their loaded muskets without even firing a shot. According to Otho Holland Williams, "The impetuosity with which they (British) advanced, firing and huzzaing, threw the whole body of the militia into such a panic, that the general threw down their loaded arms and fled, in the utmost consternation." The majority of General Caswell's North Carolina Militia likewise were swept up in the panic and, too, began to melt away as the British line surged forward. In only a matter of minutes, the Patriot left wing had almost completely collapsed. Guilford Dudley wrote of the moment, "I presently, with horror and surprise, saw the whole of our left wing falling back in confusion and dismay, throwing away their arms and all accoutrements, in order to run the swifter." In his pension statement in the 1830's, North Carolina

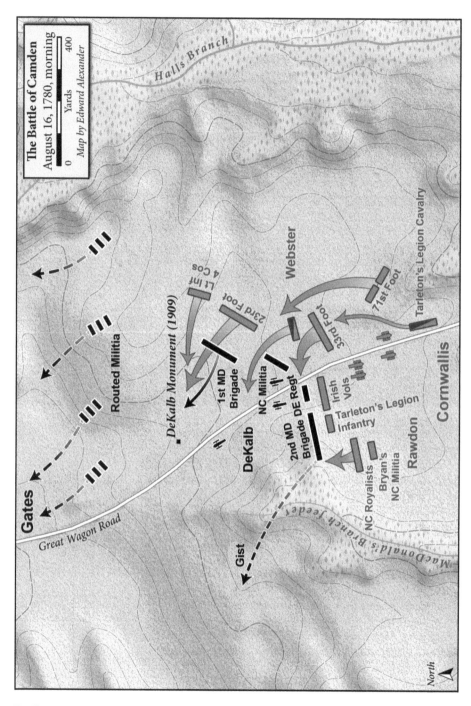

THE BATTLE OF CAMDEN, AUGUST 16, 1780, MORNING—Later in the morning on August 16, the Patriot battleline disintegrated. With the panic and retreat of the militiamen on the Patriot left, British Regulars under Lt. Col. James Webster turned left to assault the Maryland and Delaware Continentals under Baron de Kalb who were continuing to fight west of the Great Wagon Road.

militiaman Garret Watts candidly wrote: "I can state on oath that I believe my gun was the first gun fired, notwithstanding the orders, for we were close to the enemy, who appeared to maneuver in contempt of us, and I fired without thinking except that I might prevent the man opposite from killing me. The discharge and loud roar soon became general from one end of the lines to the other. Amongst other things, I confess I was amongst the first that fled. The cause of that I cannot tell, except that everyone I saw was about to do the same. It was instantaneous. There was no effort to rally, no encouragement to fight. Officers and men joined in the flight. I threw away my gun."

Later, in a letter to Virginia Governor Thomas Jefferson, General Stevens himself provided a straightforward description of the day, ". . . in short, picture it as bad as you possibly can, and it will not be as bad as it really is."

Not all the Patriot militia succumbed to the panic, however. According to several accounts, part of Brig. Gen. Isaac Gregory's brigade of North Carolinians, notably men of the 2nd Regiment commanded by Lt. Col. Henry "Hal" Dixon, stood firm along with the Maryland and Delaware Continentals just across the road. In his post-war memoirs, British Sergeant Roger Lamb of the Royal Welch Fusiliers paid homage, "In justice to the North Carolina militia, it should be remarked, that part of the brigade commanded by General Gregory acquitted themselves well; they were formed immediately on the left of the Continentals, and kept the field while they had cartridge to fire." Both Gregory and Dixon suffered severe wounds in the engagement, although both officers would survive.

Astride the Great Wagon Road, Patriot Capt. Anthony Singleton commanded two bronze 6-pounder field pieces. The fire from these guns, and others along Horatio Gates's battleline, played havoc with the British Regulars of the 23rd and 33rd Regiments of Foot during the first part of the battle. Pictured here are reproduction 6-pounders similar to the guns used at Camden on August 16, 1780. (mw)

But the damage to the Patriot line was done, and according to Otho Williams, ". . . a great majority of the militia, (at least two-thirds of the Army) fled without firing a shot."

The collapse of the Patriot left wing happened so quickly that William Smallwood's 1st Maryland Brigade, having been ordered forward to replace the charging Virginians, had not proceeded very far before the militia troops streamed back toward them and into their ranks. Like the professionally trained soldiers they were, the Marylanders calmly let the fleeing militia through and then reformed. Moving forward again they immediately engaged and began to slug it out with the troops of the 23rd and 33rd Regiments of Foot.

Hoping to find General Gates with the 1st Maryland Brigade, his aide, Major Pinckney, joined in the fight. He was later wounded and captured. Horatio Gates was not with the 1st Maryland, however. He had been swept away with the fleeing militia. Moving along the line, Guilford Dudley said he approached a North Carolina militia officer and ". . . enquired for General Gates, whom I supposed to be somewhere on the ground; the answer was, 'He's gone.' Gone where? I rejoined. 'He has fled and by this time is past Rugeley's Mills.'" In his letter to the president of Congress on August 20, Gates wrote: "General Caswell and myself, assisted by a number of officers, did all in our power to rally the broken troops, but to no purpose, for the enemy coming round the left flank of the Maryland division, completed the rout of the whole militia, who left the Continentals to oppose the enemy's whole force." Gates continued, "I endeavoured [sic] with General Caswell, to rally the militia at some distance, on an advantageous piece of ground, but the enemy's cavalry continuing to harass their rear, they ran like a torrent, and bore all before them."

Gates asserted that he continued trying to stop the hemorrhage of the militia without effect. "Hoping yet, that a few miles in the rear they might recover from their panic, and again be brought into order, I continued my endeavor, but this likewise proved in vain," he recalled, and, with "The militia having taken to the woods in all directions, I concluded, with General Caswell, to retire toward Charlotte." Not

Historical marker at the entrance to the Masonic Cemetery in Culpeper County, Virginia, on modern State Route 229, near the grave of Gen. Edward Stevens. Stevens commanded roughly 700 militiamen from Virginia at the battle of Camden. (ro)

only had the left wing of the Patriot line virtually disintegrated within the opening minutes of the fight, but in that same time the Southern Army found itself without its commanding officer as Gates spurred toward Charlotte.

After leaving Charlotte, Gates rode on to Salisbury and, ultimately, to the rallying point of Hillsborough. He accomplished this feat riding 180 miles in 3 days.

Among ensuing generations of historians, the long-perceived thought has been that Horatio Gates was keeping with a time-honored practice of posting his most experienced troops, the Continentals, on the right of the battle line at Camden, in the traditional "place of honor." If this indeed was his reasoning, then it appears he may have had nearly 25 years of military experience in the British army working against him. His formations at Camden left his green militiamen on the left to face the battled-hardened veterans of the 23rd and 33rd Regiments of Foot, for which they were no match.

While other officers distinguished themselves for gallantry in the battle of Camden, the reputation of Horatio Gates was destroyed. It would never recover.

The grave site of Gen. Edward Stevens in Culpeper County, Virginia. (ro)

BARON DeKALB
MORTALLY WOUNDED
ON THIS SPOT.
AT BATTLE OF
CAMDEN.
AUG. 16, 1780

"They Have Done All That Can Be Expected of Them"

The Collapse of the Continentals

CHAPTER SEVEN

Erected in 1909 by the Hobkirk Hill Chapter of the Daughters of the American Revolution, the De Kalb granite monument launched the preservation movement on the Camden battlefield. In 1912, the DAR accepted a donation of one acre around the monument, preserving the first piece of the battlefield. (ro)

The fighting on the west side of the Great Wagon Road was intense and, in general, was a better showing for the Patriot army. The seasoned Continentals of Delaware and Maryland were heavily engaged with the Loyalist troops of Lord Rawdon, as well as the infantry of Tarleton's Legion and, for the most part, gave better than what they got. But gun smoke hung heavy and low over the battlefield, obscuring the vision of both armies and making it almost impossible to gauge the effects of their mutual fire. According to Banastre Tarleton in his *A History of the Campaigns of 1780 and 1781, in the Southern Provinces of North America* published after the war, "The morning being hazy, the smoke hung over, and involved both armies in such a cloud, that it was difficult to see or estimate the destruction on either side."

The Continentals fought doggedly. Engaged in their front, they were unaware of the rout of the militia just across the road. Lord Rawdon's forces were pushed back during the first thirty or so minutes of the contest, losing men and artillery. It was a desperate struggle. According to Guilford Dudley, with the collapse of the militia it was the Continentals who stepped up, along with Hal Dixon's 2nd North Carolina, inflicting damage and making it hot work for the Loyalist troops. Dudley wrote: "After the recession of so large a body of the militia, the contest was renewed with redoubled vigor. The Continentals on the right of Dixon, led on by the brave De Kalb,

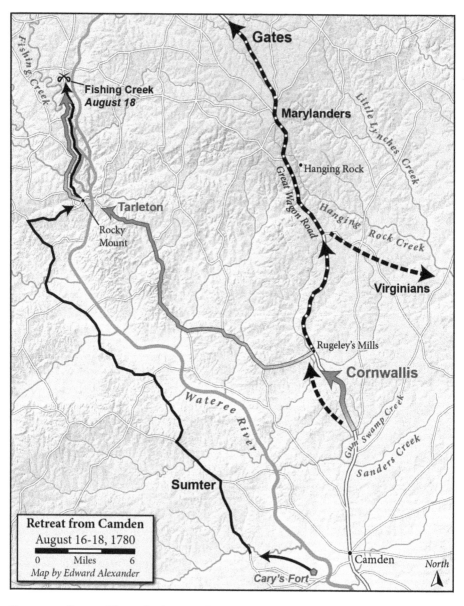

RETREAT FROM CAMDEN—The northerly route taken by the defeated Patriot forces as they escaped the slaughter of the battlefield. Also depicted is the route taken by British Lt. Col. Banastre Tarleton in his pursuit of the partisan forces of Thomas Sumter as they headed north along the west bank of the Wateree River. Tarleton was able to close the gap and give battle to Sumter's troops at Fishing Creek on August 18, 1780.

having under him Brigadiers Gist and Smallwood, never yielding an inch of ground, but on the contrary, often driving the enemy out of line."

After receiving the order to attack, Baron de Kalb immediately led his Continentals forward and engaged Lord Rawdon's forces. Even after his horse was shot out from under him, "the brave de Kalb" continued fighting on foot. His head was badly slashed by an enemy saber but was bandaged by an officer of Vaughn's Delaware Regiment. Refusing to retire, Baron de Kalb continued to fight on, leading his Maryland and Delaware boys in three separate bayonet assaults that pushed Rawdon's troops back, inflicting severe casualties on the Volunteers of Ireland. According to Otho Williams, "The second Maryland brigade, including the battalion of Delawares, on the right, were engaged with the enemy's left, which they opposed with very great firmness. They even advanced upon them, and had taken a number of prisoners." Engineering officer Lt. Col. John Christian Senf observed that the 2nd Maryland troops also captured a piece of artillery. Indeed, even Tarleton attested to the steadfastness of the American Regulars: "The action became immediately general along the front, and was contested on the left and in the center with great firmness and bravery." A pattern developed, with de Kalb's troops charging, getting pushed back, rallying again to the charge, and once more being pushed back. Though hotly engaged and suffering casualties, the well-trained and equipped British Loyalist troops were, ultimately, able to hold.

The initial position of the Maryland and Delaware Continentals, west of the Great Wagon Road on the morning of August 16, 1780. To the south and facing the Continentals were the provincial and loyalist forces of Lord Francis Rawdon, who were positioned to the left of this scene. (mw)

On the British right the Royal Welch Fusiliers, 23rd of Foot, whose service in the war dated back to Lexington and Concord in 1775, was hotly engaged, along with the 33rd Regiment and light infantry, against William Smallwood's 1st Maryland Brigade. Showing great discipline, instead of pursuing the fleeing American militia in the opening minutes of the battle the British troops focused their attention on the Continentals, pressing hard to turn the Americans' now exposed left flank. The tide began to turn.

With the increased pressure on their left, the regiments of the 1st Maryland Brigade were forced to wheel around towards the east to meet the threat, losing ground as they did so. At some point, General

West of the Great Wagon Road and looking south, the Continentals were engaged with Lord Rawdon's troops. Although wounded, Baron de Kalb led his Maryland and Delaware Continental troops on three separate bayonet charges through these woods, pushing the British provincial and loyalist troops back. An image taken in 2023 on the Camden battlefield. (mw)

Smallwood himself left the field. The brigade continued to give way, bending back towards the western part of the field, both flanks exposed, until it was nearly at a right angle to the 2nd Maryland. As a result, the left flank of the 2nd Maryland Brigade fighting near the road was now "in the air." A gap of perhaps 200 yards separated the American right and left wings.

Near the center of the action, the British 33rd Regiment of Foot was having a difficult time of it, suffering extensive casualties from the devastating canister and grape shot rounds from the "well directed fire" of the American artillery. Now, seeing the left flank of the 2nd Maryland Brigade exposed, the 33rd seized the opportunity to wheel about and apply pressure. The Patriot flank was beginning to be turned, and suddenly the 2nd Maryland Brigade was in trouble.

Otho Holland Williams, having fallen back with the 1st Maryland, saw the line of the 2nd Brigade about to give way. He galloped up furiously, trying desperately to rally the boys and get them to stand fast. Although he called for the men of his own regiment, the 6th Maryland, to hold fast it was to no avail. His call was answered by Lt. Col. Benjamin Ford, "They had done all that can be expected of them—we are outnumbered and outflanked—see the enemy charge with bayonets."

The battalions of the British 71st Regiment, Fraser's Highlanders, moved up, filling the gap between the 23rd and 33rd Regiments and creating a solid front. Lord Cornwallis at this point ordered his reserves forward. British cavalry under Maj. George Hanger charged, attacking the left flank of the 1st Maryland Brigade while Banastre Tarleton followed with the rest of his Legion dragoons. Of this moment, Tarleton enigmatically wrote, "with the remainder of his regiment, [he] completed their confusion." Most likely it was either Hanger's or Tarleton's horsemen who poured through the open gap between the 1st and 2nd Maryland Brigades, peeling off to the left and right to come sweeping in upon the rear of the Continental forces. The American artillery position was, likewise, overrun, its gun crews either shot down or captured. What remained of the Patriot battle line was now fatally compromised. The Continental regiments were being hammered on all sides and virtually surrounded.

For these Americans, the battle was lost by this juncture.

As unit cohesion broke down, the Continentals began to dissolve. Many of the men, however, continued to fight and die on the field or else surrendered. Others gathered in small groups and attempted to fight their way through the British lines. Several Continentals made their escape by fleeing into the swampy morass on their right. According to Tarleton, "Brigadier General Gist moved off with about one hundred continentals in a body, by wading through the swamp on the right of the American position, where the British cavalry could not follow."

Among the last of the American Continentals to fall was Baron de Kalb. Continuing to lead his troops, he had fought valiantly throughout the battle until wounds brought him down, forcing him out of action. He was later found on the battlefield by the British, having suffered 11 wounds in the engagement. Writing from Hillsboro a few weeks later, de Kalb's aide-de-camp, le Chevalier de Buysson, stated: "The Baron DeKalb, deserted by all the militia, who fled at the first fire, withstood with the greatest bravery, coolness and intrepidity, with the brave Marylanders alone, the furious charge of the whole British army; but superior bravery was obliged at length to yield to superior numbers, and the baron, having had his horse killed under him, fell into the hands of the enemy, pierced with eight wounds of bayonets and three musket balls. I stood by the baron during the action and shared his fate, being taken by his side, wounded in both arms and hands."

Of their captivity, de Buysson also wrote, "Lord Cornwallis and Rawdon treated us with the greatest civility. The baron, dying of his wounds two (three) days after the action, was buried with all the honors of war, and his funeral attended by all the officers of the British army." Baron de Kalb's final resting place and monument stand today in the yard of Bethesda Presbyterian Church in Camden.

With the outcome of the battle decided, Tarleton's dragoons were ordered north toward Rugeley's Mills in pursuit of their retreating foe. Here, Colonel Armand's cavalry, having fallen back

Battle of Camden and death of De Kalb.

This antiquated image depicts the destruction of the Continentals late in the battle, as the Maryland and Delaware Continentals were virtually surrounded by British infantry and cavalry forces. Baron de Kalb was wounded eleven times in this engagement, ultimately succumbing to his injuries. (nypl)

Baron de Kalb's final resting place in the church yard of Bethesda Presbyterian Church in Camden. The monument was designed by artist Robert Mills who, likewise, designed the United States Treasury Building and Washington Monument in Washington, D.C. The cornerstone of the de Kalb monument was laid in March 1825 by the Marquis de Lafayette. Engraved on the monument are the words: "Here lie the remains of Baron De Kalb, German by birth, but in principle, citizen of the world." (mw)

with the flight of the militia, attempted to make a stand but were forced to retreat. Banastre Tarleton would write: "Colonel Armand's dragoons and militia displayed a good countenance, but were soon borne down by the rapid charge of the legion. The chase again commenced . . ." Tarleton continued his pursuit for another 22 miles, halting at Hanging Rock. His forces were able to capture 150 wagons loaded with ammunition, baggage, and other supplies. Amidst the carnage and destruction of the day, at least one comical anecdote managed to emerge from this scene, and that from Tarleton's second in command, the hard charging George Hanger. "Flushed in victory and eager in pursuit," Hanger would write, "my arm was too well employed to allow much time for observation." Coming upon the baggage wagon of the dying Baron de Kalb, Hanger discovered a curious scene, "overtaking the wagon of de Kalb on which was seated a monkey fantastically dressed, I ceased to destroy and, addressing the affrighted animal, exclaimed, 'You monsieur, I perceive are a Frenchman and a gentleman. Je vous donne la parole (I give you your parole).'" Less comically, many Patriot officers and men were likewise captured in this pursuit.

The battle itself had lasted for less than an hour but the effects were felt in the South for some time to come. Lord Cornwallis reported to his superiors that Gates's army had suffered roughly 800 to 900 killed, wounded, or missing and another 1,000 captured. Although somewhat lopsided, it was not a bloodless victory for Cornwallis, whose own army suffered approximately 324 killed, wounded, or missing, including several officers. Still holding the field of battle, the British buried some of the dead of both armies in shallow, hastily dug graves. The remains of many of these brave soldiers today still lie in the sandy soil, beneath the pines, along that stretch of what was known as the Great Wagon Road. In the summer and fall of 2022, a team of archaeologists and historians unearthed the remains of 14 veterans of the battle of Camden, both British and Patriot.

The British victory at Camden was complete, and as a result the American Southern Army virtually ceased to exist for the next several months, leaving only the partisan forces of Francis Marion and Thomas Sumter to oppose Cornwallis's army. Most of the fleeing North Carolina militiamen ultimately headed for home after the rout. The Virginians, however, in unfamiliar country, mostly retraced their steps back to the rendezvous point of Hillsborough. Over the next several weeks, though, it became apparent that more of the Continental troops had survived the disaster than had first been supposed when a surprising number of them also succeeded in making their way to Charlotte. These courageous survivors of Camden went on to form the nucleus of the rebuilt American army in the south, but under a new commander. In December 1780, after he had started to rebuild the Southern Army, Horatio Gates, by order of Congress, relinquished command of the Southern Department to Maj. Gen. Nathanael Greene. General Greene remained in this post for the remainder of the war.

Lt. Gen. Charles 2nd Earl Cornwallis was a well-respected British officer known for his performance on the battlefield. His strained relationship with his commanding officer, Lt. Gen. Henry Clinton, created tension and dysfunctional communication that led to many problems for the British in the South. (nypl)

Cornwallis was well pleased with the performance of his army at Camden. He reported: "The behavior of His Majesty's troops in general was beyond all praise; It did honour to themselves & to their Country. I was particularly indebted to Col. Lord Rawdon and to Lt. Col. Webster for the distinguished courage and ability with which they conducted their respective divisions; and the Capacity and Vigour of Lt. Col. Tarleton at the head of the Cavalry deserve my highest commendations."

The valor of many officers who fought at Camden on both sides was lauded, especially that of Baron de Kalb. The same could not be said, however, of Horatio Gates. His actions after the collapse of the militia line, despite the reasoning he provided, clouded his reputation and haunted him for the remainder of his life. Charges of cowardice and ineptitude along with ridicule and disdain were raised throughout the army. In a letter to a member of Congress, Lt. Col. Alexander Hamilton of George Washington's staff, certainly not an admirer of Gates, waggishly wrote, "But was there ever an instance of a General running away as Gates has done from his whole army? And was there ever so precipitous a flight? One hundred and eighty miles in three days and a half. It does admirable credit to the activity of a man at his time of life."

Gates's detractors were not limited to men of great influence or high-ranking army officers, however, as men in the ranks could be counted among them as well. A document from one such soldier speaks volumes. On January 7, 1833, a 72-year-old man named Josiah Morton, in a petition at court, presented his claim to receive a pension for his service in the Revolutionary War. At the time a resident of Prince Edward County in

White flags mark the location where the remains of soldiers from the battle of Camden were found in the summer and fall of 2022 by battlefield archaeologists. (ro)

Virginia, Morton joined his county's militia company in January of 1780. According to his petition, Morton was among the Virginians commanded at Camden by General Stevens, and one who was able to reach Hillsborough after the rout. In describing the affair, the aged militiaman seemed quite impressed with Baron de Kalb. His opinion of Horatio Gates, however, appeared to be something else. "In this action, Baron

De Kalb perhaps the bravest man that ever lived, was killed—After the action we met in Hillsboro in North Carolina, where we were ordered to meet in the event of a Defeat. When this Declarant got there, (and he ran all the way) he here found Genl. Gates, and he hopes this may be the last time he may ever think of his name."

Peter Francisco was a legendary Portuguese soldier who immigrated to Virginia as a child. He was 6'8" and 260 pounds, and a proven fighter. At the battle of Camden, a legend grew that as the Patriots were being swept from the field, Francisco saved an artillery piece from capture by picking up the heavy tube and carrying it away on his shoulder. He is buried at Shockoe Hill Cemetery in Richmond, VA. (mw)

"In This Unguarded and Critical Moment"

The Battle of Fishing Creek

CHAPTER EIGHT

On the west bank of the Wateree River, the echo of gunfire had likely been heard early on the morning of August 16. Colonel Thomas Sumter's command of South Carolina militia, which included a small contingent of Maryland Continentals and two brass 3-pounders, moved slowly up the western shore, heading north along the river road and laden with captured wagons, supplies, livestock, and prisoners. Word of the debacle at Camden arrived later that morning. East of the river, Patriot dragoon commander Maj. William Richardson Davie had arrived in the area with his North Carolinians too late to engage in the earlier fighting near Camden. As he neared the scene of action it must have become apparent that the day had not gone well for the Patriot army. With refugees of the battle streaming past him, Davie later claimed his path was crossed by none other than Horatio Gates himself as he galloped north. According to Davie, Gates shouted for him to fall back as he expected the forces of Banastre Tarleton to be upon them at any time. "My men are accustomed to Tarleton," Davie remembered calling back, "and do not fear him." But, witnessing the confusion all about him as Gates's routed forces ran pell-mell in various directions, Maj. Davie decided that Thomas Sumter, across the Wateree, should be duly warned. With the defeat of Gates's army, Sumter's militia was now the largest organized Patriot force in South Carolina.

Reconstructed Blacksmith Shop at Historic Camden Revolutionary War site. This national historic district in the heart of Camden, South Carolina, depicts life in the South Carolina backcountry before and during the British military occupation beginning in 1780. (mw)

Born in Virginia, Sumter became a prominent landowner in South Carolina before the war. He joined the Patriot movement when his property was destroyed by the British. Leading a force of partisan fighters, he was given the nickname of "The Fighting Gamecock." (nypl)

William Richardson Davie commanded a detachment of North Carolina cavalry during the Revolutionary War. He would go on to serve as governor of North Carolina in the 1790s. (nypl)

Undoubtedly, this fact would not long escape the attention of Lord Cornwallis.

Davie dispatched Capt. Nathaniel Martin and a handful of dragoons to cross the river in search of Sumter, who was moving ever so slowly, not wishing to part with the spoils of war that had recently come his way with the capture of Cary's Fort and, as an additional bonus, an unsuspecting British supply train from the post at Ninety Six. Colonel Sumter intended to send much of the captured supplies along to Horatio Gates's army but didn't know exactly where Gates was headed. After abandoning Cary's Fort, Sumter was marching north early on August 16, back up the western shore of the Wateree, to elude any pursuers and protect his plunder, when he received word of the fate of Gates's army from William Davie's dragoons, along with instructions for him to make his way farther north toward a possible rendezvous at Charlotte some 60 miles away. According to Major Davie: "Colo Sumpter with his Detachment consisting of 100 regr infantry, a compy of Artillery, 2 brass pieces, & 700 militia began to retreat along the West bank of the river to gain the Upper Country and avoid the fate of the main Army. . . ." Although there now appeared to be more of a sense of urgency due to the apparent danger his command faced, Sumter's progress remained astonishingly slow as his militia plodded along in the sultry heat, hour after hour, with roughly 250 prisoners, numerous supply wagons, around 300 head of beef cattle, and a flock of sheep. By the evening of the 17th, the weary militiamen had reached Rocky Mount where the order was given to stop for the night. Sumter wouldn't resume his march until the next morning, August 18.

Across the river, interest in his activities was mounting. Once the major combat was over at Camden on August 16, General Cornwallis pushed his weary soldiers up to Rugeley's Mills, where he waited for Tarleton's forces to return from giving chase to American stragglers. Aware of Sumter's presence across the river, word had also reached him of the loss of Cary's Fort the previous day, as well as the supply wagons and troops from Ninety Six. Certainly, Cornwallis was eager to recover all that had been lost in the way of men and supplies as quickly as possible, and it was clear to the General that Sumter's troops posed a decided threat to the Crown's forces in South Carolina. His Lordship, however, was also keenly aware that the men of his army were exhausted. Following a nearly five-hour march along sandy roads in the sultry night air, Cornwallis's army had gone into battle early that morning. The troops

After capturing Cary's Fort, Thomas Sumter's partisan forces traveled north along the western bank of the Wateree where many of them would be captured at the battle of Fishing Creek. (mw)

needed rest, and further action would have to wait until the following day.

That action began early on August 17 with Lord Cornwallis once again dispatching the quick-moving Tarleton with orders to track down and destroy Thomas Sumter's militia. He described this move to Lord George Germain in his letter of August 21:

> *The fatigue of the troops rendered them incapable of further exertion on the day of the action; but as I saw the importance of destroying or dispersing, if possible, the corps under General Sumter, as it might prove a foundation for assembling the routed army, on the morning of the 17th I detached Lt. Colonel Tarleton with the Legion cavalry and infantry and the corps of light infantry, making in all about 350 men, with orders to attack him wherever he could find him.*

The British Legion was a Provincial regiment comprised of loyal American troops from the New York area. The regiment consisted of both elite infantry and cavalry troops. Wearing green coats, the dragoons were ferocious in battle and known as Tarleton's Green Horse. (rd)

Likewise, Cornwallis issued orders to Lt. Col. George Turnbull and Maj. Patrick Ferguson, whose Loyalist troops were "at that time on Little River," to move east from near Ninety Six to "pursue and endeavour to attack General Sumter."

Upon receiving his orders, Banastre Tarleton set out after Sumter with his British Legion, light infantry troops from the 71st Regiment of Foot, and a 3-pounder fieldpiece. He moved north along the east bank of the Wateree River up to the Catawba. With his usual alacrity, the Green Dragoon doggedly pushed his troops 30 miles along the river in the extreme heat. By dusk, the British had reached the ferry crossing at Rocky Mount. Across the river, Tarleton could make out the campfires of Sumter's men flickering in the darkening sky. He ordered his own tired troops to encamp but with no fires to be lit, as he waited silently to see if Sumter would cross back to the eastern side of the river where he intended to ambush the Patriots. By some means, Sumter had learned of Cornwallis's orders to Turnbull and Ferguson to try to cut him off. By marching north, he had eluded that threat so far, but he had received no intelligence regarding Tarleton. That would change presently.

By the early morning of August 18, Thomas Sumter had at last received word of the danger across the river. He ordered his troops to resume their march but remained on the western shore. The heat was stifling and Sumter's men neared exhaustion. By noon, crossing Fishing Creek, which flowed east into the confluence of the Wateree and Catawba Rivers, Sumter ordered a halt. According to William Richardson Davie's account, "He marched again at daybreak—and about 12 o'clock the detachment halted having passed Fishing Creek and gained an open ridge on the No side of the creek, the Detachment halted in the line of march, the rear guard consisting of militia were posted at the creek." Somehow, incredibly, Thomas Sumter was under the mistaken belief that he was out of Tarleton's reach and safe from pursuit. After marching only eight miles that morning, he incautiously allowed his men to make camp and rest.

Tarleton's troops crossed the river to Rocky Mount and began their march up the western bank behind Sumter. Due to the heat and the extreme pace set by their commander, the men of the Legion Infantry companies were nearly spent by the time they reached the banks of Fishing Creek around noon. Not wanting to risk having his quarry escape, Tarleton made the decision to press on with a smaller number of troops who were still fit to continue the chase. He later wrote:

As a lieutenant colonel, Banastre Tarleton commanded a legion (infantry and cavalry) under Lord Cornwallis and built a reputation for brutality on and off the southern battlefields. With a much smaller force, he won a decisive victory over Thomas Sumter's forces at Fishing Creek on August 18, 1780. (loc)

> *When Tarleton arrived at Fishing Creek at twelve o'clock, he found the greatest part of his command overpowered with fatigue; the corps could no longer be moved forwards in a compact and serviceable state: He therefore determined to separate his cavalry and infantry most able to bear farther hardship, to follow the enemy, whilst the remainder, with the three pounder, took post on an advantageous piece of ground, in order to refresh themselves, and cover the retreat in case of accident. The Number selected to continue the pursuit did not exceed one hundred legion dragoons and sixty foot soldiers.*

With the light infantry troops of the 71st of Foot riding double behind the Legion dragoons, Tarleton's pursuit of Sumter's militia continued in earnest, now with a pared down strike force of just 160 men.

North of Fishing Creek, after posting sentries, Sumter encamped along the river road about halfway between the creek and the Catawba River. There were ravines to the north and south, and thus it seemed a good position. The Continentals of the 5th Maryland

Regiment stacked their arms and Sumter's exhausted men began to kindle cook fires. Some slept in the shade under the wagons while others waded out into the cool water of the river. Many of them helped themselves to peaches from a nearby orchard owned by a local Tory named Reaves. Several more indulged in a captured store of rum and soon were roaring drunk. Sumter posted more sentries along the ravines, then pulled off his coat and boots and settled down on a blanket under a wagon for some much-needed rest. It was clear he had no inclination of the approaching danger. According to William Richardson Davie:

> *The prisoners and part of the baggage were in the advance guard, the troops were permitted to stack their arms and indulge themselves in rest or refreshment, several strolled to a neighboring plantation, some went to the river to bathe, and numbers sought in sleep some refuge from their fatigue, in this unguarded and critical moment, Col. Tarleton approached the American Camp.*

Tarleton's force crossed Fishing Creek, and according to their commander, "This detachment moved forwards with great circumspection: No intelligence, except the recent tracks upon the road, occurred for five miles." Writing of the incident in 1848, however, the Reverend James Hodge Saye of South Carolina disagreed. Attributing his account to "the late William Ashe of Franklin County, Ga., who was at the time with Sumter," Saye affirmed that Tarleton had indeed gained some intelligence regarding Sumter's camp and disposition from some local Tories:

> *It happened that two Tory women passed the place soon after Sumter had come. They had passed the rear guard about half a mile when they met Tarleton's force. They gave Tarleton precise information as to Sumter's position and the arrangement of things connected with his army. They also informed him of a way by which he could leave the main road and fall into a road leading to Sumter's position at right angles to the main road. This way was taken by the British and hence came upon wholly unexpected.*

Given the situation that existed between the Whig and Tory population in South Carolina at the time, it is certainly feasible that Tarleton could have

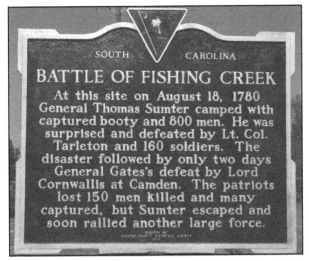

SOUTH   CAROLINA

BATTLE OF FISHING CREEK
At this site on August 18, 1780
General Thomas Sumter camped with
captured booty and 800 men. He was
surprised and defeated by Lt. Col.
Tarleton and 160 soldiers. The
disaster followed by only two days
General Gates's defeat by Lord
Cornwallis at Camden. The patriots
lost 150 men killed and many
captured, but Sumter escaped and
soon rallied another large force.

This marker detailing the
August 18, 1780 battle fought
nearby, is located near
Great Falls, South Carolina,
in Chester County, at the
intersection of US 21 and
Waterview Drive. (mw)

received such reports from local Tories about Sumter's encampment and the position of his troops. The South Carolina backcountry absolutely witnessed acts of civil war that was every bit as contentious as anything that would occur in the American South of the 1860s.

Tarleton sent an advance force under Capt. Charles Campbell of the 71st galloping ahead. Rounding a bend they came upon Sumter's two sentries at the creek who immediately opened fire, killing one of the dragoons. In a fury, the Green Horse charged with slashing sabers; the Patriot militiamen were savagely cut down and hacked to death. Up ahead in the American encampment, Thomas Sumter roused from his sleep after hearing the report of the sentries' muskets and was told it was some of the men shooting at cattle for meat.

Moving along a high ridge between the creek and the river, the British advance suddenly halted and signaled for Tarleton, who wrote: "Tarleton rode forward to the advanced guard, and plainly discovered over the crest of the hill the front of the American camp, perfectly quiet and not the least alarmed by the vedettes." As Tarleton looked down upon the quiet American camp, he saw muskets stacked to one side and unalarmed men taking their ease. He wasted no time in forming his troops for battle. "The decision, and the preparation for the attack, were momentary," he recalled, and "The cavalry and infantry were formed into one line, and, giving a general shout, advanced to the charge." All at once, in what must have seemed like an instant, the late peaceful American camp was plunged into chaos and confusion as Tarleton's Green Horse and the Light Infantry Corps charged into the camp to secure the stacked weapons before the Patriot troops could muster. "Universal consternation immediately ensued throughout the camp; some opposition was, however, made from behind the wagons, in front of the militia," Tarleton wrote. Having heard the earlier shots from the sentries, Patriot Col. Edward Lacey had formed his troops behind the wagons. The militiamen here were able to put up some resistance, but it was only momentary. Among the rest of Sumter's surprised army, terror and panic spread quickly as the British forces swept down upon the camp.

Tarleton later wrote that the artillery and stacked arms of the Continentals were rapidly secured. Many of the Continentals of the 5th Maryland were cut down by the Green Horse as they tried to retrieve their weapons. Their commander, Lt. Col. Charles Woolford, was likewise badly wounded. Many of Sumter's men, having been in the rum stores, were so drunk they were unable to resist Tarleton's troops. In a matter of minutes all semblance of resistance was at an end as Americans fled in all directions, many of them brutally cut down as they tried to make their escape.

With the sudden charge of the British Legion, Thomas Sumter awoke from his slumber. All around him he saw chaos throughout his camp. His troops in a panic, with many of them being struck down and cut to pieces before his eyes, Sumter mounted a horse and rode out bareback to try to rally them, but to no avail. Bootless and in a state of undress, he made the decision to make his own escape into the woods. He had not gone far when a low-hanging tree branch knocked him from his horse, rendering him senseless as he lay sprawled on the ground. Unnoticed by the British, Sumter roused himself a few minutes later, remounted his horse, and made good his escape. A few days later, he joined the forces of William Richardson Davie in his camp.

Colonel Thomas Taylor, the former Virginian who had led Sumter's forces in the successful attack on Cary's Fort only a few days before, was severely wounded in the engagement by a saber cut across his head. Unarmed, he fell to the ground, initially playing dead. Later, fearing that he would be hanged, he smeared blood and mud over his face to keep from being recognized as an officer, and when rounded up was held with the other prisoners. In a moment of confusion during their march back to Camden Taylor, along with Lt. Col. Henry Hampton, managed to make a successful escape by darting into the woods, apparently undetected by the British. Many other captured militiamen escaped in much the same way.

At Fishing Creek, in just a matter of minutes, Banastre Tarleton's small force killed or wounded 150 Patriot soldiers and captured another 310, including all the Continental troops of the 5th Maryland. The British also captured 44 wagons, 1,000 pieces of small arms, both American cannon, and numerous horses. Likewise, Tarleton successfully freed the 250 prisoners who had been in Sumter's possession at the time of the battle. The victory, however, came at a price; Capt. Charles Campbell, 71st Highlanders, who had led Tarleton's advance guard, was killed in the action. "Captain Charles Campbell, who commanded the light infantry, was unfortunately killed near the end of the affair," Tarleton wrote. "His death cannot be mentioned without regret." As for the British Legion, the losses were almost negligible, "fifteen non-commissioned officers and men, and twenty horses, were killed and wounded." Tarleton's victory at Fishing Creek was complete.

With his escape, Thomas Sumter lived to fight another day. Recovering from his loss, in astonishingly quick fashion he was able to reassemble a new fighting force and, along with other partisan leaders such as Francis Marion, engage in an ongoing series of harassing actions against the British forces remaining in the South. He would also avenge his humiliating defeat at Fishing Creek, exacting a price from Banastre Tarleton. On November 20, 1780, at Blackstock's Plantation, Sumter's forces stopped Tarleton's British Legion, handing the Green Dragoon his first defeat in the war. Because of the stubborn ferocity of his tactics, Tarleton would say of Thomas Sumter that he "fought like a gamecock." From that day forward, Col. Thomas Sumter was known as the Fighting Gamecock.

British High Tide

EPILOGUE

On August 19, 1780, just three days after the American debacle at Camden, Patriot militia forces engaged British Provincial and Loyalist troops at Musgrove Mill, at an important fording place on the Enoree River. Among the Patriot militia forces engaged were frontier riflemen under the command of Col. Isaac Shelby. In the slang of the times, these were men "with the bark on." (mw)

In the wee hours of August 16, 1780, two armies incredibly bumped into one another on a white sandy road in the South Carolina backcountry. Major General Horatio Gates, flushed with what he considered his own success at Saratoga in 1777, hoped to replicate that success as he led his Grand Army of Patriot soldiers south towards the British stronghold at Camden. Comprised of tough, well-trained Continental troops from Maryland and Delaware, and a small contingent of light infantry and cavalry augmented with roughly 2,000 militiamen from North Carolina and Virginia, Gates appeared confident as he marched on that humid early morning. Perhaps, though, he was somewhat overconfident. He had fewer rank-and-file troops than he originally thought but, in his own words, "these are enough for our purposes." What was his intention?

After receiving a report from engineering officer Lt. Col. John Christian Seft, it appeared that instead of marching his army from his encampment at Rugeley's Mills with the purpose of directly attacking the British garrison at Camden, Horatio Gates was deploying his forces to Sanders Creek. In his after-action report to Congress, Gates said he resolved to ". . . take post in an Advantageous Situation, with a deep creek in front, about seven miles from Camden." If he could establish a strong defensive position on the north bank of the creek, perhaps Gates could entice the British into an ill-advised attack.

In Camden and commanding all British forces in the southern theatre was Lt. Gen. Earl Cornwallis. Only recently arrived at the outlying post from Charleston, Cornwallis took the position of immediately attacking the American Southern army at their encampment at Rugeley's Mills in order to alleviate this threat to his army. In a report to London, Lord Cornwallis stated that "seeing so little to lose by a defeat, and much to gain by a victory, I resolved to take the first good opportunity to attack the rebel army."

Coincidentally, both the Patriot and British armies set off on their march at about the same time, 10:00 p.m. on the night of August 15. After marching along the Great Wagon Road for hours in the humid night air, at about 2:30 a.m. on the morning of the 16th, the unthinkable happened. The vanguards of the two armies literally blundered into one another on the road. Amid great confusion, shots were exchanged and after a few tense moments both sides settled down to await the break of day.

At dawn, the battle commenced. Lasting less than one hour, the ensuing combat all but destroyed the Patriot army. Positioning his ill-experienced militiamen on the left flank, east of the Great Wagon Road, Horatio Gates pitted these untested soldiers against the cream of the British army, the 23rd and 33rd Regiments of Foot. Within moments of the opening shots, many of these militiamen fled in terror, throwing away their loaded muskets as they ran. Caught up in this mad rush was none other than Maj. Gen. Horatio Gates himself.

West of the road on the Patriot right flank were the Maryland and Continental regiments of the 2nd Maryland Brigade. Under the direction of Maj. Gen. Johann, Baron de Kalb these Patriots troops were up against well trained, and battle tested British Provincial and Loyalist troops commanded by Lord Francis Rawdon. While the Continental troops more than held their own, the rout of the Patriot militia on the left all but sealed the fate of the Southern American army. Virtually surrounded by the British assault force, the Maryland and Delaware Continentals were all but annihilated.

Suffice it to say that August 16, 1780, turned out much differently than the confident Horatio Gates anticipated. Along with the loss of the Southern army as an in tact fighting force, Gates also lost something perhaps more precious to him: his military reputation.

As most of the militia forces retreated in the opening minutes of the battle, Gates later claimed that he was swept up in the rush. In his report to Congress, it was stated that the general was attempting to rally the panicked militia but to no avail. Seeing the enemy coming around the flank, Gates said he "endeavored to rally the militia at some distance, on an advantageous piece of ground, but the enemy's cavalry continuing to harass their rear, they ran like a torrent, and bore all before them." Thinking the battle was lost, Gates asserted that he decided to fall back, with other officers, to Charlotte. He rode on to Salisbury and then to the rallying point of Hillsborough. Gates made this 180-mile ride in just 3 days. Charges of ineptitude and even cowardice were levelled; with it, the reputation of Horatio Gates was destroyed.

For all intents and purposes, the rout of the American Patriot forces at Camden was catastrophic, rendering the Southern American Army, albeit briefly, defunct. For the British forces under the command of Lt. Gen. Earl Cornwallis, it was a brilliant beginning to a campaign he hoped would lead to total victory in the South and render a death blow to the American revolutionary cause. Frustratingly for the Crown, however, that death blow proved quite elusive. As events unfolded in the coming months, it became clear that the Patriot debacle at Camden was not the beginning of the end for the American war effort, but rather the reverse. The battle of Camden ultimately constituted the high tide for British military success in the Southern American theater.

Just days after the losses at Camden and Fishing Creek, a small Patriot victory at Musgrove Mill set the stage for what was to come. Located in the South Carolina backcountry of Laurens County near a main ford along the Enoree River, Henry Musgrove's gristmill was a key site for the local grain supplies. The British had recently established an outpost at the mill to guard the river ford, garrisoned by around 200 loyalist troops. On August 17, 1780, Patriot militia Col. Charles McDowell sent a like number of mounted militia troops, men from South Carolina, Georgia, and what is now Tennessee, to attack the garrison at Musgrove Mill and secure the ford. Under the command of Cols. Isaac Shelby, Elijah Clarke, and James Williams, the Patriot force arrived near the mill and encamped on the night of August 18.

Born in Maryland in 1750, Isaac Shelby served in Lord Dunmore's War and fought at the battle of Point Pleasant in 1774. In 1780, living on the frontier of what is now eastern Tennessee, Shelby led a force of riflemen at the battle of Musgrove Mill. In response to British Maj. Patrick Ferguson's threat to "hang their leaders and lay waste to their country with fire and sword," Shelby's troops, along with other frontier forces known as the Overmountain Men, joined with southern militiamen to soundly defeat Ferguson's provincial forces at Kings Mountain on October 7, 1780. (nypl)

After sending out a small reconnaissance force the next day, the Patriot commanders were dismayed to learn that the British had been substantially reinforced. The scouts brought back news obtained from a local farmer that over 100 Tory militia had apparently joined the garrison at the ford, along with approximately 200 British provincial troops. Now, with a fighting force of around 500, the British garrison at Musgrove Mill outnumbered their opponents considerably. The Patriot troops found themselves caught between a rock and a hard place. A frontal assault was now out of the question based on the sheer numbers of those opposing them. Also, with their horses worn out, the Patriot commanders knew they would be unable to effect a rapid withdrawal to avoid battle. With their presence discovered by a British patrol, the element of surprise was now lost as well. Finding themselves out of better options, the Patriot leaders made the decision to fight where they stood.

On a ridge overlooking the road to the mill, the Patriots hastily threw up a defensive breastwork. Using a tactic often seen on the frontier from Native American warriors, a small force under the command of Capt. Shadrach Inman of Clarke's Georgia militia was sent forward. Inman intended to engage the Tory troops and then immediately fall back, hoping to lure the enemy forward into a clever ambush. The plan worked like a charm. The Tories, commanded by the Scotsman Col. Alexander Innes, took the bait. As the Georgia militiamen fell back, Innes's loyalists hotly pursued. The Patriot forces behind the breastwork were ordered to hold their fire until they could "distinguish the buttons" on the clothing of the enemy troops. At less than 100 yards, the Patriot militia opened fire with devastating effect.

The well-trained loyalists rallied, however, continuing to press on. With fixed bayonets, Innes's men turned their attention to the American right flank, occupied by Isaac Shelby's frontier riflemen. Lacking bayonets themselves, Shelby's men initially fled before the loyalists' assault. With the Patriot line weakened, Elijah Clarke again ordered his Georgians forward, attacking the right flank of the loyalists. Also, about this time, one of Shelby's riflemen drew a bead on Col. Innes. The shot was true, and Innes tumbled from his saddle with a serious wound. With their commander down, the Tory attack stalled. Isaac Shelby's frontiersmen then returned to the fight, pouring deadly and accurate rifle fire into the loyalist ranks. With the continuous pressure from the Patriot line, the loyalist troops faltered and fell back into what, initially, was an orderly withdrawal. As the Patriot militiamen increased the intensity of their fire, the withdrawal developed into a headlong rout. The fight was over; it was a short one, lasting around one hour. Although successful at Musgrove Mill and in possession of the field, the Patriot commanders made the decision to disperse their troops after learning of the defeat of Horatio Gates at Camden three days earlier.

Francis Marion was commissioned a Brig. Gen. of South Carolina troops by Governor John Rutledge. Unlike Thomas Sumter, Francis Marion, a former Continental officer himself, worked well with Continental units such as the Legion of Lt. Col. Henry "Light Horse Harry" Lee. (nypl)

After losing nearly his entire command at Fishing Creek on August 18, 1780, Patriot militia colonel Sumter, the Gamecock, recruited a new and sizable fighting force of nearly 1,000 men. Similar to Lt. Col. Francis Marion, known as the Swamp Fox, Sumter began a harassing partisan campaign against the occupying British force in South Carolina that managed to cause His Majesty's forces much consternation.

The partisans for the most part were usually well mounted and moved swiftly to disrupt British lines of supply and communication with their hit-and-run tactics. When pursued by the enemy, the partisans simply melted away into the countryside. They were home-grown, South Carolina boys mainly, who knew the terrain and were habituated to the hunting life. Through skirmishes with the Native American peoples of the area, namely the Cherokee, these men were accustomed to frontier weapons and battle tactics. The situation in the South Carolina backcountry was almost tailor-made for irregular warfare. For many months, these partisan operations were the mainstay of the Patriot war effort in the South. While other successful partisan leaders emerged, such as Elijah Clarke and Andrew Pickens, it was the efforts of Francis Marion and Thomas Sumter that arguably constituted the highest threat to the British occupation of South Carolina. Indeed, Lord Cornwallis called Thomas Sumter his "greatest plague." In November 1780, after failing to ride down the forces of Francis Marion in a 26-mile chase, the hated British Colonel Tarleton said of Marion, "as for this damned old fox, the Devil himself could not catch him." Marion was later commissioned a brigadier general of state troops by South Carolina Governor John Rutledge.

By the end of 1780, Lord Cornwallis found his efforts to move into North Carolina curtailed greatly, as a good portion of his command was constantly kept busy chasing Patriot guerrilla forces. When American General Nathanael Greene relieved Horatio Gates as commander of the Southern Army in December, he prudently included the partisan forces in his overall strategic plan for the coming campaign. Unlike Thomas Sumter, Francis Marion tended to work well with the Continental Army. Along with the Regulars of Lt. Col. Henry "Light Horse Harry" Lee's Legion, in April 1781, Brig. Gen. Marion succeeded in capturing Fort Watson, on the Santee River. In May, along the Congaree, his siege operations were successful in reducing the British supply depot at Fort Motte.

As Cornwallis moved into North Carolina, his left flank was protected by a force of American loyalist militia under the command of Maj. Patrick Ferguson. Since September Ferguson, known in the British army as the Bull Dog, had been busy recruiting Tory troops in the South Carolina backcountry. He was equally anxious to discourage local men from joining the Patriot cause. After the battle of Musgrove Mill, Col. Isaac Shelby led his frontier militia force back across the Appalachian Mountains to the Watauga Settlement, in what is now eastern Tennessee. In a gross misjudgment, hoping to dishearten these men and cow them into remaining neutral going forward, Ferguson issued a stern proclamation. Sending the message through a released Patriot prisoner, Ferguson ordered the frontiersmen to "desist from their opposition to British arms" or else he would "march over the mountains, hang their leaders, and lay their country to waste with fire and sword." Patrick Ferguson lived just long enough to regret this brazen act of intimidation. In response to the proclamation, on September 25, 1780, at Sycamore Shoals in modern east Tennessee, frontiersmen from west of the mountains rendezvoused with men of North Carolina, South Carolina, and Virginia. Mustering under leaders such as Isaac Shelby, John Sevier, William Campbell, Benjamin Cleveland, and Joseph McDowell, this frontier army of Overmountain Men and southern militia began their march southeast to confront Ferguson's force. Ultimately numbering around 1,400, the army was nominally commanded by the Virginian William Campbell.

Learning of the approach of this frontier force from Patriot deserters, Patrick Ferguson wisely made the decision to fall back from his camp at Gilbert Town

Virginian Henry Lee III commanded a legion of Patriot infantry and cavalry troops throughout the Revolutionary War. Using guerrilla tactics and known for the boldness and speed of their attacks, Lee's Legion certainly rivaled the British Legion, earning for its commander the nickname of "Light Horse Harry." After the war, Henry Lee served as governor of Virginia and, delivering a eulogy at the funeral of George Washington in 1799, described the president as "first in war, first in peace, and first in the hearts of his countrymen." Lee was also the first American historian of the Southern American Campaign in the Revolutionary War. (nypl)

Maj. Patrick Ferguson was a Scottish officer serving in the British forces. He was an expert marksman and designed an early breechloading rifle. Leading a force of provincial and loyalist forces in the North and South Carolina backcountry as part of Lord Cornwallis's command, he was killed in action at Kings Mountain on October 7, 1780. His forces were defeated there by southern Patriot militiamen and frontier riflemen known as the Overmountain Men. (nps)

to Charlotte, where Lord Cornwallis commanded the main British force. He also sent a request for reinforcements that, unfortunately for him, did not reach Cornwallis until after the coming battle. On October 4, the Overmountain Men reached Gilbert Town where they were joined by a small number of Georgia militiamen. At the grazing site known locally in the South Carolina backcountry as Hannah's Cowpens, the Patriots received word on October 6 that Ferguson's force was just ahead of them, heading east. The frontiersmen quickened their pace.

At this point Ferguson, rather than pushing on to Charlotte, made the unwise decision to occupy a forested, rocky hill called Kings Mountain on the border of North and South Carolina. With his loyalist troops numbering around 1,200, and believing he held the advantage by holding the high ground, Ferguson encamped at the pinnacle of Kings Mountain and awaited the arrival of the Overmountain Men. He then sent a second request to Lord Cornwallis for help. In order to reach Ferguson quickly, around 900 mounted Patriot militiamen rode through the night of October 6, fording the Broad River early on the morning of the 7th, still several miles from Kings Mountain. By the early afternoon, however, the frontiersmen had reached Ferguson's position. Surrounding the hill, they launched an all-out attack from all sides. William Campbell told his men to "shout like Hell and fight like devils."

During the battle, the well-trained loyalist provincial troops mounted several bayonet assaults that managed to drive the frontiersmen back down the hill, only to have them return to the fight, keeping up their deadly rifle fire. Throughout the waning afternoon, Ferguson's defensive perimeter was ever shrinking. One loyalist remembered that the Overmountain Men "looked like devils from the infernal regions . . . tall, raw-boned, sinewy with long matted hair." Attempting to break through the Patriot ranks, Patrick Ferguson led a last-ditch charge. Mounted and conspicuous in his checkered battle shirt, with his right arm dangling uselessly at his side from a severe wound he had received at the battle of Brandywine in 1777, the young Scotsman made an easy target for the

well-armed frontiersmen. Hit with multiple gunshots, Ferguson died of his wounds and was buried on the site where he lies today. With their commander dead, the loyalists were forced to surrender. Lord Cornwallis had lost his left flank protection. From Charlotte, he fell back into South Carolina, delaying still further his invasion of North Carolina. Other setbacks were to follow, with the backcountry coming more and more under Patriot control. In an attempt to curtail the resurgence of Patriot sentiment in South Carolina, Cornwallis ordered Banastre Tarleton to cease his fruitless chase of the Swamp Fox, Marion, and focus his efforts on disrupting the activities of his "greatest plague," Thomas Sumter.

This antiquated image depicts Maj. Patrick Ferguson as he was killed attempting to break through the Patriot lines with his men at the battle of Kings Mountain on October 7, 1780. (nypl)

After his death at the battle of Kings Mountain on October 7, 1780, the commander of the British Provincial troops, Maj. Patrick Ferguson, was buried by his men on the battlefield. The present monument was dedicated in 1930 for the 150th anniversary of the battle. (rd)

With the recent British defeats, loyalist sentiment in the backcountry began to wane. Cornwallis hoped to buoy the confidence of the local Tories.

With his own British Legion and the infantry of Lt. John Money's 63rd Regiment of Foot, Banastre Tarleton set out in pursuit of Sumter in the latter part of November 1780, moving up the Enoree River. In a stratagem that had proved successful for him at Fishing Creek back in August, Tarleton again divided his forces, leaving his foot soldiers and artillery behind while he pushed on with his Legion dragoons and mounted infantry. With about 270 men, Tarleton's stratagem focused solely on closing the gap with Sumter. This time around, however, the Gamecock was ready for him. After running before Tarleton for two days, Sumter, now a brigadier general, made the decision to turn and take up a good, defensible position in order to receive the British advance. In present-day Union County, South Carolina, on rolling hills above the Tyger River, Sumter formed his defense on the farm of William Blackstock. The farmhouse and outbuildings there were solidly constructed of logs which were unchinked, providing openings from which men could fire from cover. The farm fields surrounding the buildings were cleared, giving the Partisans open, unobstructed fields of fire.

Sumter posted Col. Henry Hampton's South Carolina riflemen inside the farm buildings. He

Many of Thomas Sumter's partisan troops took up positions in and around the outbuildings and fences at the home of William Blackstock as they defended themselves against the forces of Lt. Col. Banastre Tarleton on November 20, 1780. It was a Patriot victory but, more importantly, it marked the first time during the war that Tarleton's British Legion was stopped and defeated. (mw)

This historical marker, describing the battle of Blackstock's Plantation on November 20, 1780, is located at the Battle of Blackstock's Historic Site in Union, South Carolina. (lks)

Located at the Battle of Blackstock's Historic Site in Union, South Carolina, this monument marks the approximate site where Brig. Gen. Thomas Sumter defeated the forces of British Lt. Col. Banastre Tarleton on November 20, 1780. (lks)

dispersed more troops along a heavy rail fence on the left and in thick woods to the right of the house, with the Tyger River at their rear. Down a slight slope to their front, close to the farm fields, around 100 Georgia militiamen under Col. John Twiggs established a skirmish line. Late in the afternoon of November 20, 1780, Banastre Tarleton's force appeared. In his usual style, Tarleton made the decision to come straight ahead, ordering his 270 troops into an all-out frontal assault against Sumter's 1,000 militiamen. Initially, the tactic appeared to be working as Twigg's Georgians fired too soon and were unable to reload before they were hit by a bayonet charge from Lieutenant Money's 63rd Regiment of Foot. As a result, the Georgians were on the run back up the slope toward the farm buildings, with Money's troops in hot pursuit. Advancing too far, however, the men of the 63rd found themselves in trouble, coming under heavy fire from Henry Hampton's riflemen in the farm buildings. They began taking heavy losses; Lieutenant Money and two of his officers were killed in this charge. Moving around and through the woods on the right, Patriot Col. Edward Lacy advanced his mounted riflemen near a detachment of Tarleton's dragoons, who were not in the fight but merely watching Money's attack. Lacy opened up on the unsuspecting dragoons with a brisk fire at point-blank range. Though under fire and beginning to take losses, the disciplined troopers of the Green Horse were able to recover enough to drive Lacy's horsemen off with a saber charge. By all appearances, Tarleton's quick thrust against the Patriot militia was coming undone.

By this juncture, in desperation and believing now that the battle was going against him, the previously undefeated Tarleton ordered his cavalry to charge the Patriot infantry position, uphill, and into the waiting ranks of Sumter's riflemen. The outcome of this injudicious charge was predictable; British dragoons tumbled from their saddles in droves. The lane leading to the house and farm buildings was strewn with the bodies of dead men and horses. The British charge was broken, though Tarleton's troops were able to withdraw in good order. With things appearing to be going his way, Thomas Sumter and his staff at this point exposed themselves to harm, imprudently riding up to watch the action. The Patriot officers were scattered by a volley fired from men of the British 63rd, however. Sumter himself was severely wounded from this fire and would be out of action for the next several months. He relinquished command to Col. John Twiggs, who held his position for several hours after the firing died down. Tarleton's forces fell back about two miles and encamped for the night, with Tarleton fully intending to resume the battle in the morning. He would be disappointed in this venture, however. Deceptively leaving his campfires burning, John Twiggs withdrew from the Patriot position at Blackstock's and forded the Tyger River during the night. The fight was over.

British losses at Blackstock's Plantation were considerable; 92 killed and around 100 wounded. American losses were slight, less than 10 killed or wounded and another 50 or so captured during the combat. The outcome of this battle was significant, though; Tarleton's British Legion as a whole was stopped and defeated. It was Banastre Tarleton's first defeat of the war.

What had begun so well for the British Army in the South with that quick, decisive victory at Camden three months before, was slowly turning into a logistical nightmare for Lord Cornwallis. He was consistently stymied by partisan Patriot forces intent on keeping his army pinned down in South Carolina. While he ultimately managed to move north, reaching Virginia in May 1781, Cornwallis's once promising campaign in the South came to an end for him at Yorktown.

While the battle of Camden in August 1780 all but destroyed the Southern army, enough of that force survived to form the nucleus of the rebuilt Southern army under Maj. Gen. Nathanael Greene. By wars end, the British presence in South Carolina was confined to the city of Charleston.

Located at the Battle of Blackstock's Historic Site in Union, SC, on this hillside, near the Tyger River, stood the house and farm buildings of William Blackstock. On November 20, 1780, Patriot Thomas Sumter, the Gamecock, positioned his militiamen in and around these buildings and handed the British Legion of Banastre Tarleton its first defeat in the Revolutionary War. (lks)

The white granite monument stands atop Battleground Ridge at Kings Mountain National Military Park in Blacksburg, South Carolina. (rd)

"Their Immortal Honour Made a Brave Defense"

APPENDIX A

PHILLIP GREENWALT

Sitting on horseback upon the heights of Brooklyn and peering across the marshes toward Long Island, Gen. George Washington watched the unfolding engagement. During the height of the battle Washington supposedly exclaimed in desperation, "Good God! What brave fellows I must lose this day." Trapped on the other side was the 1st Maryland Regiment under the command of Col. William Smallwood. These resolute Continentals were expertly covering the retreat of the army against the closing jaws of the advancing British forces. To buy time for their fellow comrades to manage the crossing, 4 companies of the 1st Maryland, approximately 400 men, charged into the 2nd Grenadiers and 71st Highlander Regiments of the British army. In all, the Marylanders charged into five times their number. One historian described the battle of Long Island and the heroics of the Marylanders as "An hour more precious to liberty than any other in history."

Ten of them made it back to friendly lines. Over 250 were killed or mortally wounded and another 100 wounded and or captured. The other companies, along with the approximately 35 men that were fit for service, returned from Brooklyn after the smoke cleared. These men formed the nucleus for a regiment that desperately needed to be reconstituted. Through the ensuing years of the war, Washington came to count on these Marylanders, and when another crisis loomed for the American cause in 1780, the regiment was called forward to respond.

The Marylanders who bled at Long Island first mustered in earlier that year. On January 14, 1776, the Maryland Regiment was formed to fulfill the quota of troops assigned to the state by the Continental Congress. Initially consisting of nine companies, eight being regular infantry and one of light infantry, the regiment was assigned to service with the main

The Maryland Line of the Continental Army is honored through many monuments. The Maryland Line Monument in Baltimore was erected in 1901 by the Maryland Society of the Sons of the American Revolution. It reads "To all patriots of Maryland who during the Revolutionary War aided on land or at sea in gaining the independence of this state and of these United States and to the Maryland Line the Bayonets of the Continental Army." (loc)

Continental army on July 6 of that same year. In the intervening months, between recruitment and assignment, the Marylanders drilled and trained. Eventually they arrived at Washington's camp in New York, a well-drilled and well-supplied unit. At the end of their muskets were bayonets, a rarity at that junction in the war for the Continentals.

Their service in the American Revolution, one could argue, was fitting of the term elite. Or on par with future units in American military history. The coming years of the conflict could attest to that moniker.

The regiment was in New York approximately two weeks before they showed their grit when they covered the retreat of Brig. Gen. William Stirling's brigade from Long Island on August 27, 1776. The regiment continued to see active service in all the major battles and campaigns: from the slog through wintry weather to the battles at Trenton and Princeton, to the slugfest at Brandywine, to the near victory at Germantown, and through the heat of Monmouth in June of 1778.

When disaster struck American hopes in the southern theater with the surrender of Charleston, South Carolina in May 1780, and with it the loss of the entire southern Continental army, a decision had to be made. Washington knew he needed to send forces from his main army to reverse British success in the southern colonies. The Virginian knew exactly who to send. On April 2, 1780, Washington wrote to the Continental Congress about the "weak state of our *force* there [southern theater] and unhappily in this quarter also, have laid me under great embarrassments, with respect to the conduct that ought to be pursued." Knowing he faced the expiration of service of approximately a quarter of his army, the disaster in the south had to be rectified. He thusly sent his best to be the core of a new Continental army. The Maryland Line, along with their Delaware compatriots, headed south.

Three days later, on April 5, 1780, the decision became fact when the orders were issued and the Marylanders and Delaware soldiers broke camp and began their trek south under the command of Maj. Gen. Baron Johann de Kalb. This force consisted of the two Maryland regiments, the 1st and 2nd, along with the Delaware Continentals.

Who were the men that tramped south, behind leaders such as de Kalb, Brig. Gen. William Smallwood, Col. Otho Holland Williams, and Maj. John Eager

Howard, names that have become synonymous with the southern theater?

Although most of what we know about the Marylanders comes from information collected by Brig. Gen. William Smallwood in 1782 while he mustered in recruits for Maj. Gen. Nathanael Greene's army, some of this data gives us insight into several of the men who hastened south in the spring of 1780. The return lists 299 men for which the following conclusions can be made. Extrapolating data from the records available, Edward C. Papenfuse, longtime Maryland State Archivist and historian, and author Gregory A. Stiverson wrote in 1973 that Smallwood's 1782 recruits "were probably typical of other Maryland men who fought as privates in the war."

Most of the Marylanders that comprised these 299 were foreign born, many of whom hailed from England or Ireland. Only 79 recruits simply listed "America" as their place of origin. In terms of age, native born soldiers, Maryland or "America," were between the ages of 14 and 29. Of the 299, 145 listed their ages between that range at enlistment. Another 22 were listed between the ages of 25 and 29. However, for foreign born enlistees, two-thirds of the 120 gave their ages as between 25 and 39 years of age. Professions of enlistees varied widely. Tax returns and assessments point to the fact that most privates in the Maryland Continental Line were newly freed servants, free laborers, or the sons of poor farmers, with the bounties offered and basic needs met (food, pay, uniform) as enticements for joining. Even data from a unit raised in 1776 from Maryland reflected these findings, with laborers and tradesmen being prevalent pre-war occupations.

Whether born in the colony of Maryland or across the Atlantic Ocean, the men of the Maryland units marched south wearing a uniform coat of blue faced with red trim, long overalls, and waistcoats of white linen. At least that is what was proscribed by

GOOD GOD! WHAT BRAVE FELLOWS
I MVST THIS DAY LOSE
GEORGE WASHINGTON

Today, the Maryland Monument at Prospect Park in New York City honors the Maryland 400 who fought at the battle of Long Island. The inscription reflects Washington's feelings on the Maryland Continentals. (nycdpr)

The battle of Eutaw Springs on September 8, 1781, was the last major battle of the war in the South. Like most battles before, the Maryland Continentals were in the thick of the fight and performed admirably. (nypl)

Washington in 1779 in general orders. By the spring of 1780, however, there was most likely a mixture of hunting shirts of homespun interspersed among the men along with various footwear. The general orders of the same time do not explicitly detail the headwear the Marylanders donned. A smoothbore musket, to which a bayonet could be affixed, was carried on the shoulder as these resolute veterans marched into North Carolina.

When Maj. Gen. Horatio Gates arrived in the southern theater to take command of the reformed Continental army, his objective was to advance into South Carolina. The Marylanders went with him. After accidentally bumping into the British advance north of the town of Camden, South Carolina on the night of August 15, the Marylanders proved their mettle in a brief nighttime skirmish. When Continental cavalry stampeded after running into the advance of the British, the Marylanders held their position as an advance infantry unit and "executed their orders gallantly." Later that same morning, other Marylanders did the same on the field of Camden. But would their mettle be enough for the American cause that day?

As Gates unfolded his army, one regiment of Marylanders was assigned a position on the extreme right flank while the other, the 1st Maryland, was assigned a place in reserve in the middle of the American formation. Both units suffered grievously, along with their Delaware comrades, in the debacle at Camden. The panic that ensued on the American left flank was beyond their vision. These men, with service dating back to 1776, methodically loaded and fired, listened to their officers, and slowly gained ground, twice repulsing British advances, cutting down "half the number" in one enemy company and "two-thirds" in another.

These men "had the keen edge of sensibility rubbed off by strict discipline and hard service until their left flank became uncovered." Flanked, their minds turned to survival. The man who had led them south, de Kalb, fell mortally wounded. More fell into British hands.

Despite their appalling losses at Camden, some Marylanders remained in the ranks while others rejoined the two regiments as they were rescued from captivity by South Carolina partisans. At least 20 of the men in the 1st Maryland who had fought and survived Long Island in 1776 stood ready to move out on March 15, 1781, at Guilford Court House in North Carolina, ready to defend an army and keep open a route of retreat. For some of these men in the 1st Maryland, their length of service ranged as high as 94 months. Imagine the commitment and survival of these "brave fellows."

An Irishman and transplanted Virginian serving on the staff of General Gates summed up what Washington and others already knew about the mettle and professionalism of the Marylanders. After he witnessed the carnage at the battle of Camden, Maj. Charles Magil penned:

> *The men, to their Immortal Honour made a brave defense, but were at last obliged to give ground and were almost all killed or taken; Gist's Brigade behaved like heroes, so did Smallwood's. But their being more to our left afforded us no opportunity of saving them . . .*

Another Maryland officer who later reflected on the battle of Camden felt "confident upon equal ground we could have fought, and I think subdued an equal number of the British troops." That spirit, after such a devastating reverse in South Carolina, is a fitting epitaph on the make-up, determination, and professionalism of the Marylanders that served with during the American Revolutionary War.

Washington needed them. Gates's army survived because of them. Greene would need them. The Marylanders were one of the best military lines in the service of America. A fitting and living example of the soon-to-be state nickname, "The Old Line State."

PHILLIP S. GREENWALT is the co-founder of Emerging Revolutionary War and a full-time contributor to Emerging Civil War. He is the author or co-author of two volumes of the Emerging Revolutionary War Series. He is currently a supervisory park ranger for the National Park Service in Maryland.

Colonial Militia

APPENDIX B
ERIC WILLIAMS

Since the earliest days of England's colonization of the New World, conflict stalked the new settlements. Land disputes with tribal communities of various indigenous peoples often led to war throughout the seventeenth and eighteenth centuries. At the same time, many European powers, especially France, eyed America as a favorable place to extend their own empires. For British colonists in America, their first line of defense was the militia.

Most towns or settlements within the colonies established military or militia companies, comprised of local inhabitants who turned out in times of emergency, and often acted as an auxiliary to the regular military forces of Great Britain. When the danger passed, the militia returned to their homes and private lives. Though there were exceptions, generally all able-bodied men between the ages of 16 and 60 were required to serve in a militia company.

Most volunteer recruits went through a quick physical "exam" to ensure they had an adequate number of teeth, were disease-free, and were able to shoulder a firearm. Militia service could also be a colony's form of tax payment. Training was sometimes conducted by a man who had prior military experience. Drilling was often done under shade trees or at a community's "common" or open grassy area. The "captain's" knowledge of how to handle, load, and fire a musket or artillery was imparted to the men through seemingly endless drilling, memorizing manuals of arms, keeping clean their firearms, and maintaining accoutrements like cartridge boxes and sometimes bayonets.

By the mid-seventeenth century, militia commanders in Massachusetts organized smaller companies of men, taken from the ranks of the town militias, who could act as first responders in times of danger. Commanders were ordered "to make a choice of thirty soldiers of their companies in ye hundred,

By late 1780, the backcountry of South Carolina was the scene of many atrocities between Whig and Loyalist fighters. Many of these men were neighbors before the war. Some were even friends. But politics of the day, plus mounting animosities and old scores to settle turned the backcountry into a bleeding ground of civil war. (mw)

Along with the frontiersmen from what is today eastern Tennessee, called the Overmountain Men, came militia companies from Virginia, North Carolina, and South Carolina. Many of these men were habituated to the outdoor, frontier life of hunting. They were, as some called them, "men with the bark on." (rd)

who shall be ready at half an hour's warning." Later, on the verge of hostilities with the Wampanoag people led by King Philip, militia companies were ordered to "be ready on a moment's warning, to prevent such danger as may seem to threaten us." Eventually, these smaller units came to be known as "minute companies." Generally, minute companies were comprised of younger men, 30 years of age or younger, who were quick, agile, and kept ready for rapid deployment. They were citizen soldiers who were required to be ready "in a minute's notice". By the 1750's, during the French and Indian War, some companies began calling themselves "minutemen". While all minutemen were part of the militia, not all militia troops were minutemen. On average, minutemen made up only about a quarter of a militia company.

Although an ocean apart, by the latter half of the eighteenth century, England felt confident in its dominion over the thirteen American colonies. Largely unnoticed however, after decades of forging a living in the harsh new world, English settlers eventually took

Patriot militiamen often brought differing types of arms with them when they marched off to war. In the South Carolina backcountry particularly, one could see British long pattern muskets, known as the Brown Bess, French style Charlevilles, and often the uniquely American long rifle. (nps)

on a feeling of independence. By the time of the American Revolution, England was forced to expend much time, treasure, and military power to hold the rebellious thirteen who had declared independence from the Crown's orbit.

Throughout the American Revolution, local militias were used on both sides of the conflict, with the British army recruiting loyalist units to augment their Regular forces and Patriot commanders routinely calling upon local Whig militia companies to support the more well-trained and battle-hardened American Continental troops. In most Revolutionary War battles the use of local militias supporting or opposing British control was well-documented. The battle of Camden on August 16, 1780, is a prime example of the use of both Loyalist and Patriot militia units and, for the most part, their performances in this fight were in striking contrast with one another.

Typically, American militiamen, whether Patriot or Loyalist, came from all walks of life. They were farmers, tailors, and blacksmiths. Many had served in the French and Indian War twenty years before. When hostilities between Britain and her American colonies broke out in the 1770s, many of these men brought their old weapons and battered equipment again to war. (ca)

On the Patriot side, militia companies from Virginia and North Carolina lined up alongside the hard-bitten Continentals from Maryland and Delaware. Most of these militiamen were green, poorly equipped, and poorly trained. Indeed, in the opening moments of the battle, as the seasoned British Regulars of the 23rd and 33rd Regiments of Foot approached, huzzaing with muskets aslant and fixed bayonets, most of the Patriot militia fled the field, many throwing away their loaded muskets. In minutes, the Patriot left wing had virtually collapsed.

The story was different on the Patriot right where the Continentals were facing very well-trained Loyalist militia and provincial troops from New York and North Carolina. Although suffering casualties, the Loyalist troops in the end were able to stand firm. Though pushed back at times during the battle, their lines did not break. Ultimately, with the rout of the Patriot militia, the American Continentals were surrounded by British Regulars and Loyalist forces and cut to pieces.

With the defeat of the Southern Army at Camden, partisan fighters and militia, ably led by Brig. Gen. Thomas Sumter and Brig. Gen. Francis Marion,

Living historians play a valuable part with educating the public on what a Colonial-era militiaman wore plus equipment and weapons he used. Here is a living historian portraying a Patriot militiaman demonstrating how a smoothbore musket is primed before the cartridge is loaded. (mw)

rose up and for many months constituted the largest contingent of Patriot resistance. They likewise confounded the best efforts by the British Army to pacify the South Carolina backcountry.

During the war, particularly in the backcountry, feelings for and against the King at times got bitter. Bill Cunningham was a famous Loyalist commander who at times exacted revenge on those who did not openly support the King. He was known to wield his sword in the process and often drew blood, earning himself quite a reputation.

Patriot militia commanders often defended their men's abilities and put their faith and trust in them. Patriot commander Andrew Pickens, also a legend in South Carolina, was a trustworthy leader whom his militia troops readily followed. There exist many stories of Loyalist and Patriot commanders who were neighbors and who once shared friendships before the war. Hostilities turned these men against each other. Such was the case with militia soldiers whose passionate beliefs were divided by the war. Hard feelings between backcountry residents lingered for generations.

Throughout the remainder of 1780 and into 1781, Patriot militias made a better showing. Just days after the fight at Camden, well-led American Patriot militia soundly defeated their Loyalist American counterparts at Musgrove Mill. In October 1780, southern Patriot militia units from Virginia, North Carolina, South Carolina, and Georgia joined with frontiersmen known as the Overmountain Men. These additional forces came from what is today east Tennessee. The Overmountain Men, in addition to the aforementioned Patriot militia units, defeated the Loyalist provincial troops of British Maj. Patrick Ferguson at Kings Mountain.

At Blackstock's Plantation on November 20, 1780, Patriot partisan commander Thomas Sumter handed Lt. Col. Banastre Tarleton and the Loyalist troops under his command their first defeat of the war. This green-coated British Legion and their commander, known for their ruthlessness, were previously undefeated until this engagement.

Probably most famously, in January 1781, southern Patriot militiamen joined with Continental troops under the Virginian Brig. Gen. Daniel Morgan. These combined troops won a decided victory at the battle of Cowpens. Once again, Banastre Tarleton felt the sting of defeat.

Throughout the American Revolution, local militia companies, whether Patriot or Loyalist, routinely turned out in times of emergency, rising to the support of both the American Continental and Regular British army forces. As the war continued, however, with their forces bogged down in South Carolina, British commanders consistently overestimated the number of militia soldiers who were "loyal to the king". They became frustrated by what they considered a lack of support. Conversely, by war's end it was the Patriot militia forces, at times a hindrance, that ultimately proved to be an essential part of the overall American success in the fight for independence.

Eric K. Williams is a retired National Park Service Ranger/ Historian with a lifelong interest in early American history. He continues to write on historical topics and presents living history programs. He and his wife, Jan, live in Greenwood, South Carolina.

"SWAMP FOX"

SACRED TO THE MEMORY OF
BRIG. GEN. FRANCIS MARION
WHO DEPARTED THIS LIFE, ON THE 27th OF
FEBRUARY, 1795, IN THE SIXTY-THIRD YEAR OF HIS
AGE; DEEPLY REGRETTED BY ALL HIS FELLOW
CITIZENS.

HISTORY
WILL RECORD HIS WORTH, AND RISING
GENERATIONS EMBALM HIS MEMORY, AS ONE OF
THE MOST DISTINGUISHED PATRIOTS AND HEROES
OF THE AMERICAN REVOLUTION: WHICH ELEVATED
HIS NATIVE COUNTRY

TO HONOUR AND INDEPENDENCE,
AND
SECURED TO HER THE BLESSINGS OF
LIBERTY AND PEACE.
THIS TRIBUTE OF VENERATION AND GRATITUDE IS
ERECTED IN COMMEMORATION OF THE NOBLE
AND DISINTERESTED VIRTUES OF THE
CITIZEN;
AND THE GALLANT EXPLOITS OF THE
SOLDIER;
WHO LIVED WITHOUT FEAR, AND DIED WITHOUT
REPROACH.

Partisan Leaders

APPENDIX C
ROBERT M. DUNKERLY

"Nothing but blood and slaughter has prevailed among the Whigs and Tories, and their inveteracy against each other must, if it continues, depopulate this part of the country."
— Nathanael Greene

When the British took over control of South Carolina in the summer of 1780, the existing state militia system (and government) collapsed. Loyalists who had been suppressed and laid low for the last five years rose up and organized themselves to join the British occupiers. With no Continental troops in the state, into the vacuum stepped local militias and partisans to sustain the American war effort.

Several leaders emerged whose talents and natural abilities allowed them to effectively organize and manage the resistance to the British and Loyalists. Most recognizable are what we'll call the big three: Marion, Sumter, and Pickens. Each happened to operate in a different part of the state, and each had talents and strengths the others did not.

Francis Marion was the only one of the trio native to South Carolina. Born into a wealthy planter family, he resided in Berkeley County. As a captain in the 2nd South Carolina, Marion fought at Fort Moultrie in one of the first American victories of the war. He also participated in the failed attempt to recapture Savannah in 1779 and avoided capture in Charleston while recovering from an injury. In the summer of 1780, Francis Marion began his partisan operations, successfully battling British and Loyalist forces in the low country. Returning to his plantation after the war and serving in the state Senate, Francis Marion died in 1795 at the age of 67.

Thomas Sumter was born in Hanover County, Virginia. As a young man he was in Braddock's March in the French and Indian War. Moving to South Carolina he married Mary Jameson and lived at the High Hills of Santee.

Partisan units became vital to the Continental effort in South Carolina. They frequently partnered with regular Continental forces to attack British units. In April 1781, Marion's forces worked with Col. Henry "Light Horse Harry" Lee to capture the stockade at Fort Watson, cutting a major supply line from Charleston to Camden. (ro)

Marion's men used their knowledge of the creeks, swamps and back roads to attack isolated British units and supply columns. They traveled light to allow for quick strikes. From December 1780 to March 1781, Marion's men established a base camp at Snow's Island along the Pee Dee River. (nypl)

When war broke out, Sumter organized a local militia unit. He was later elected lieutenant colonel of the 2nd South Carolina Regiment. When the state fell to the British, he led militia as a brigadier general. Sumter was aggressive and inspiring, yet often led costly attacks. He also preferred independent command to cooperating with the Continental army.

After the war Sumter served in the House of Representatives and in the Senate. He was the longest living Continental general, passing away in 1832 at age 97. Fort Sumter in Charleston harbor is named for him.

Andrew Pickens was born in Bucks County, Pennsylvania, near Philadelphia. His family joined the migration down the Great Wagon Road and settled in South Carolina. He moved to the frontier, settling near the Georgia border, started a farm and established a trading post for the Cherokee.

At the start of the war Pickens fought in campaigns against local loyalists in the western part of the state. He also fought at Kettle Creek in Georgia. Captured when Charleston fell, he agreed to sit out the war. When his property was damaged by the British, he felt his oath was no longer valid and actively joined the resistance.

Pickens fought at Cowpens, Augusta, Ninety Six, and in various campaigns against the Cherokee on the frontier. His knowledge of Indian culture and respect among the Cherokee earned him the nickname Skyagunsta, "The Wizard Owl". After the war Pickens was a legislator in the state House of Representatives, a delegate to the Constitutional Convention, and served in Congress. He died in 1817 and is buried in the town of Clemson.

South Carolina had been free of British troops and under American control until the spring of 1780, when British forces invaded and captured Charleston. Then came British victories at the Waxhaws and Camden. It was at the former that the British, especially Lt. Col. Banastre Tarleton, acquired a reputation for cruelty.

Sumter was operating just north of Camden and captured a supply train of wagons and many prisoners. Stopping to rest at Fishing Creek, British cavalry under Tarleton surprised and routed Sumter's force. The Americans lost 150 killed and about 300 captured, and Sumter himself barely escaped.

That summer Sumter led aggressive attacks on British posts at Hanging Rock and Rocky Mount, both of which failed to dislodge the defenders. British forces struck back at him at Fishdam Ford and Blackstock's, and under his leadership the Americans held their ground.

In the meantime, Francis Marion, still recovering from an injury to his ankle, began to recruit men for guerrilla raids. Starting with about 20, he soon had 70 followers. Operating in the sparsely settled lower counties of the state, they spied, attacked convoys, and disrupted the recruitment of loyalists. British General Cornwallis said of Marion, "there was scarcely an inhabitant between the Santee and the Pee Dee that was not in arms against us."

Tarleton set out to destroy Marion's force in November 1780, and the partisan earned the nickname "old swamp fox". After a futile effort in the swamps of the lower part of the state, Tarleton wrote that as for this "damned old fox the Devil himself could not catch him." His knowledge of the region and contacts among the local population enabled his forces to elude capture and strike at will.

In January 1781 at the battle of Cowpens, Pickens commanded the militia in a crucial part of the battle.

Though known as a hero of South Carolina, Thomas Sumter was born in central Virginia in 1734. His father was an indentured servant and his mother a midwife. Sumter served in the Virginia militia and fought in the French and Indian War as well as other Indian expeditions until he migrated to South Carolina due to issues with debt in Virginia. (ro)

This early twentieth century print commemorates several Patriot military heroes of South Carolina, including partisan leaders Marion, Sumter, and Pickens. These men are still honored today through names of towns counties, colleges, and highways. (nypl)

Following his instructions to fire and fall back calmly, the militia on the front line lured the British into a trap.

That summer General Sumter used a controversial tactic to recruit troops, known as Sumter's Law. He offered slaves and confiscated loyalist property as bounty for men to join his brigade of State Troops. The effort brought in recruits but had lukewarm support from the state government. It helped fuel the passions in an already brutal civil war in the region.

Pickens's militia assisted in the siege of Ninety Six that summer, conducted by Maj. Gen. Nathanael Greene's Continental troops. Greene asked Sumter to block British reinforcements, but Sumter preferred to attack a British fort, and with Ninety Six reinforced, Greene had to withdraw. It was one example of Sumter's independent streak.

The big three never fought in a battle together, although their troops did. In September 1781, Sumter was ill, but his brigade of State Troops joined the forces of Marion and Pickens and other militia to fight with the Continental army at Eutaw Springs. Pickens was wounded in the action.

Ironically, none of the big three fought at the most famous and significant partisan battle in the state, Kings Mountain. Most of the American force here were militia from North Carolina, Virginia, and the Overmountain (modern Tennessee) settlements.

The 2000 film, *The Patriot*, blends characteristics of all of the big three in its fictional main character, Benjamin Martin. The film also combines elements of the battles of Cowpens and Guilford Courthouse in its final battle scene.

Aside from the big three, a number of other competent leaders emerged in South Carolina.

Colonel William Hill resided in the New Acquisition District, in the upper part of the state. He led troops that fought at Kings Mountain, Hanging Rock, Williamson's Plantation and later in battles under Sumter. His grandson was Confederate D. H. Hill.

Wade Hampton was a wealthy plantation owner who served as a captain in the 2nd South Carolina Regiment, then after the war served in Congress. His grandson was a Confederate cavalry general.

Colonel William Bratton led militia from the New Acquisition District, fighting at Kings Mountain and other battles in the region. Later in the war he was a Colonel in Sumter's brigade.

Edward Lacy of the New Acquisition District led troops in 1780 and 1781, rising to the rank of colonel. He fought at Kings Mountain, Rocky Mount, Hanging Rock, Fishing Creek and other battles in the upcountry.

While the actions of the big three, Francis Marion, Thomas Sumter, and Andrew Pickens, were certainly instrumental to the success of the American Patriot cause, it is equally important to remember the contributions of the other commanders who likewise fought in the southern theatre, as well as the common soldiers, who truly stepped up in the summer of 1780 at a time when all looked lost.

Robert M. (Bert) Dunkerly *is the author of* Unhappy Catastrophes: The Revolution in Central New Jersey, 1776–1782 *in the Emerging Revolutionary War series.*

WAXHAW PRESBYTERIAN CHURCH
ORGANIZED 1755 BY SCOTCH-IRISH.

THE FIRST CHURCH IN UPPER SO. CAR.
THIS 4½ ACRE TRACT WAS DEEDED TO
THE CONGREGATION BY ROBERT MILLER
SCHOOL-TEACHER AND MINISTER, MAR. 9, 1758.
THE FIRST PASTOR WAS
REV. WM. RICHARDSON, 1759-1771.
THE EARLIEST BUILDING OF LOGS WAS USED
AS A HOSPITAL FOR WOUNDED SOLDIERS
DURING THE REVOLUTIONARY WAR
AND WAS BURNED BY THE BRITISH.
THIS, THE FOURTH, WAS BUILT IN 1896
AND REMODELED IN 1942.

ERECTED BY
WAXHAWS CHAPTER, D.A.R.
1948

South Carolina Backcountry Summer 1780 Tour

APPENDIX D

With the fall of Charleston in May 1780, Patriot resistance fell to the many small partisan militia bands throughout South Carolina. The British established outposts, manned by a mix of Regular and Provincial troops along with Loyalist militia. The war in South Carolina became a brutal civil war between neighbors, friends, and families who found themselves on opposite sides. This tour will take you to some of the places that were part of the backcountry fighting that led up to, and continued after, the battle of Camden. Some sites are well marked and are publicly accessible historic sites, while others are unmarked.

Buford Battleground (Battle of Waxhaws)

262 Rocky River Rd, Lancaster, SC 29720

This small park commemorates the battle of Waxhaws (May 29, 1780) between Col. Abraham Buford's 400 Virginia Continentals and Lt. Col. Banastre Tarleton's 150 strong British Legion. The battle ended in a rout of Buford's forces that Patriot leaders at the time called "Buford's Massacre." The impact of the battle wiped out all organized Patriot forces in South Carolina, but also became a rallying cry for Patriot partisan leaders in South Carolina. The first monument was placed here in 1860 at the site of a mass burial of battlefield dead (Buford lost an estimated 113 men killed). There are several other memorials and interpretive signage around the park. The American Battlefield Trust and South Carolina Battleground Preservation Trust have worked to preserve more land than the current park (which is managed by the Lancaster County Parks and Recreation Department). Additional trails are planned, and the site is part of the Liberty Trail.

Waxhaws Presbyterian Church monument is located on Old Hickory Road in Lancaster, South Carolina. The church was first organized in 1755. The original church building was constructed of logs and used as a hospital for soldiers wounded in the battle of the Waxhaws on May 29, 1780. (ro)

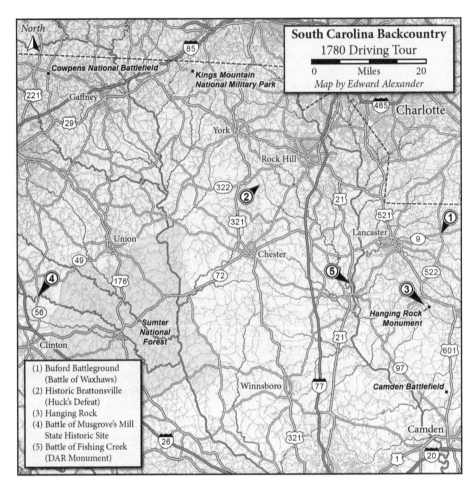

SOUTH CAROLINA BACKCOUNTRY 1780 DRIVING TOUR—The war in South Carolina was a legitimate "civil war" among neighbors and families. The brutality and guerrilla-style warfare played havoc on the ability of the Crown's forces to subjugate the state. Though a major victory, the capture of Charleston gave the British a false sense of success and hope in their upcoming campaigns in South Carolina.

The Waxhaws Liberty Trail marker is located near modern Lancaster, South Carolina, and stands as part of the commemoration of the battle of Waxhaws, fought on May 29, 1780. The engagement was between British forces led by Lt. Col. Banastre Tarleton and Virginian Abraham Buford. The site is part of the South Carolina Liberty Trail. (ro)

Historic Brattonsville (Huck's Defeat)

1444 Brattonsville Rd, McConnells, SC 29726

Historic Brattonsville is an 800-acre historic site that interprets 18th and 19th century history of the South Carolina Piedmont. Nearly 30 historic structures are preserved and interpreted via costumed interpreters. The site focuses on historic agriculture, foodways, and day to day life of the Brattonsville community. The site served as one of the filming locations for the movie *The Patriot*.

The historic William Bratton House still stands today, and, it was here that Bratton's wife Martha was threatened by British officers on the whereabouts of her husband, a known Patriot militia leader. Martha got

The Huck's Defeat Trail takes visitors on an interpretive walk through the area where Capt. Christian Huck's forces were annihilated by Patriot militia, inspiring a rally call to others across the South Carolina backcountry. (sj)

word to her husband of the arrival of the British via a slave named Watt (buried on the property today). As Watt rode to inform Bratton of the oncoming danger, the mixed force of British Legion and Loyalist militia set up camp at the nearby Williamson Plantation. Their leader, Capt. Christian Huck, forced Martha Bratton to fix him and his officers dinner before restraining her and her family to her home. William Bratton was able to get a force of about 250 militia and attacked Huck's 120 men force at Williamson Plantation on July 12, 1780. The short battle ended in a total defeat for the British with only an estimated 24 men escaping. Captain Huck was mortally wounded in the battle. The site of Williamson's Plantation and the battle is preserved as part of Historic Brattonsville and an interpretive trail leads east from the Bratton House to the battlefield. The small but important battle further emboldened the Patriot militia throughout South Carolina.

Hanging Rock

GPS: 34°34'14.1"N 80°40'34.8"W

Here, at this small pull off, is the center of the Hanging Rock Battlefield with Liberty Trail signage. The Hanging Rock Battlefield is a recent preservation success story, with various preservation groups purchasing battlefield property and placing easements on other land.

There were two battles here at Hanging Rock, one fought on July 30, 1780 and the other on August 6, 1780. In July, a North Carolina Patriot force under Maj. William Davie attempted to attack the British post at Hanging Rock while Col. Thomas Sumter's forces attacked the British post at Rocky Mount, west of Hanging Rock. Davie's sortie was to prevent the British at Hanging Rock from reenforcing the British at Rocky Mount. Davie quickly realized the British force under Col. Samuel Bryan was too large for his 80 mounted men, so instead he ambushed a

Preservation efforts at the Hanging Rock battlefield site have led to opening the battlefield to public access and interpretation. As of 2023, the site is under development and is part of the Liberty Trail. (ro)

smaller detachment of North Carolina Loyalists north of the main British force. Davie routed the small Loyalist force.

On August 6, Sumter's combined forced of 800 militia (mostly mounted) attacked the British outpost at Hanging Rock under Maj. John Carden. Carden's force consisted of 1400 Loyalist militia and Provincials. Starting north near Hanging Rock Creek, Sumter again routed Davie's North Carolina Loyalist camp located to the west on Beecher Horton Road (historic Catawba River Road). Sumter then moved southward and attacked the British Provincial camp located here at the intersection of Beecher Horton and Flat Rock Roads. The momentum of Sumter's attack shocked the Provincials in camp and after heavy fighting, they fled southward down Flat Rock Road. Many of Sumter's men became undisciplined and looted the British camps, allowing the next camp of the Prince of Wales Regiment to put up a stand and establish a hollow square against the Patriot horsemen (located approximately at GPS: 34°33'52.7"N 80°40'20.3"W—private property, do not trespass). Portions of the British Legion also assisted in slowing down Sumter's advance. Though Sumter's forces were able to inflict 200 casualties and capture supplies, he was not able to follow up on his initial success due to British stubbornness, the exhaustion of his men, and their undisciplined looting of the British camps. Sumter pulled back to the north and Carden's forces eventually joined the main British force in Camden.

A young 13-year-old Andrew Jackson of nearby Waxhaws served with the Patriot militia by assisting with watching the horses and other small support duties. Jackson and his brother were later captured in 1781 and held captive in Camden.

Nearby on South Carolina State Park land is the geographic feature "Hanging Rock." Also, there is a monument placed by the Daughters of the American Revolution to the battle of Hanging Rock. Though the actual battle took place west of here, the monument does mark the actual location of the "hanging rock." The monument and "Hanging Rock" are located at GPS: 34°33'55.8"N 80°39'43.6"W, with the monument in front of, and below, the rock formation.

Battle of Musgrove's Mill State Historic Site

398 State Park Rd, Clinton, SC 29325

The Musgrove Mill State Historic Site encompasses nearly 400 acres with 2 ½ miles of interpretive trails and a museum/visitor center dedicated to the battle of Musgrove Mill that was fought on August 19, 1780. There is also access to the Enoree River for kayaks and canoes.

The battle of Musgrove Mill was fought three days after the American disaster at Camden. Patriot militia attempted to attack a Loyalist camp near a ford across the Enoree River. The Patriot force consisted of a mixture of South Carolina, North Carolina, and Georgia militia. Militia leaders believed the Loyalist camp only included approximately 200 men (the same as their force) but soon found out that they were recently reenforced by 300 men (including Provincial Regulars) from Ninety Six. Finding out too late to call off the attack, the American militia "fortified" behind a makeshift barrier of logs and brush. The Loyalists, though outnumbering the Patriot forces, charged the militia's position. The Americans were

Located at 398 State Park Road, Clinton, South Carolina, this site commemorates the battle of Musgrove Mill fought on August 19, 1780, between Patriot militia leaders Isaac Shelby, Elijah Clark, and James Williams and British provincial and loyalist troops. The battle came just three days after the devastating defeat of Gates at Camden. (ro)

able to repulse the attack and then counter attacked, scattering the Loyalist and British forces. Within an hour, the Americans lost only 16 men while the mixed force of Loyalists and Provincials lost 63 killed and 70 captured. The victory further proved that Loyalists and British Provincials had a hard time keeping control of the South Carolina backcountry.

The enthusiasm of the victory was tampered when news of Gates's defeat at Camden reached the militia. Instead of following up their small victory with an assault on Ninety Six, the force broke up with many crossing to the western side of the Appalachian Mountains. Many of these units participated in the battle of King's Mountain two months later.

Battle of Fishing Creek (DAR Monument)

Corner of US 21 and SC 733, Great Falls, SC
GPS: 34°37'24.6"N 80°54'05.0"W

This small monument, placed by the Daughters of the American Revolution in 1930, marks the approximate location of the battle of Fishing Creek. Most historians believe Gen. Thomas Sumter's camp was near where Fishing Creek met the Catawba River (today Fishing Creek Lake/Reservoir). One mile north on the right is a state historic marker for the battle of Fishing Creek.

On August 18, two days after the battle of Camden, General Sumter's camp of 800 partisan soldiers were quickly overrun by 160 men of the British

A marker for the battle of Fishing Creek can be found on U.S. Highway 21 (Catawba River Road), near Great Falls, South Carolina. It commemorates the battle fought there on August 18, 1780, between South Carolina partisan troops under Thomas Sumter and British cavalry and light infantry under Banastre Tarleton. The British surprised and all but decimated Sumter's force. (mw)

Launched in 2019, the Liberty Trail—developed through a partnership between the American Battlefield Trust and the South Carolina Battleground Trust—connects battlefields across South Carolina and tells the captivating and inspiring stories of this transformative chapter of American history. (ro)

Legion under Lt. Col Banastre Tarleton. Sumter was caught by surprise and lost nearly 150 men killed, 300 captured, and many stores that Sumter captured at Cary's Fort a few days earlier. Tarleton suffered only 16 casualties. Sumter's forces were completely scattered.

Gates's Road to Camden

APPENDIX E

On this tour you will be following the main route of Gates's "Grand Army" using primary sources and correspondence from the time. Not all the original roads used in 1780 are still in use, so modern routes that generally follow the historic routes are used. Gates, against the opinions of most of his officers, chose this route as the most direct and fastest to Camden. This area in 1780 was mostly barren and provided little provisions for the army. The sandhills, long leaf pine, and wiregrass ecosystem was not well suited for growing foodstuffs. The nearby Carolina Sandhills National Wildlife Refuge is a great place to learn about the historic geography and ecosystem of this region. Gates's army was already poorly fed and equipped when they left Cox's Mill in North Carolina; this landscape worsened their condition.

The stops on this tour are mostly unmarked with no interpretation. Many are on private property so please use caution and do not trespass beyond your vehicle. We have made an effort to provide at each stop a place for a vehicle to pull over. Take caution as you drive as many roads are two lane rural roads.

Stop 1—Cox's Mill/ Buffalo Ford

GPS: 35°40'32.5"N 79°37'10.2"W

The pull off is at the crossroads of Parks Crossroads Church Road and NC Route 22. This entire area was used by Baron de Kalb's Continentals for their encampment in July 1780.

Baron de Kalb, sent by General Washington from New Jersey to reenforce Charleston, commanded some of the best Continental soldiers in the American army. A mixed force of Maryland and Delaware Continentals, de Kalb and his men were not able

Thanks to the efforts of local, state, and federal officials as well as local preservation groups, most of the Camden battlefield is preserved. As of 2023, new signage and trails are installed as well as parking and programming. The battlefield is part of the South Carolina Liberty Trail in conjunction with the American Battlefield Trust. (ro)

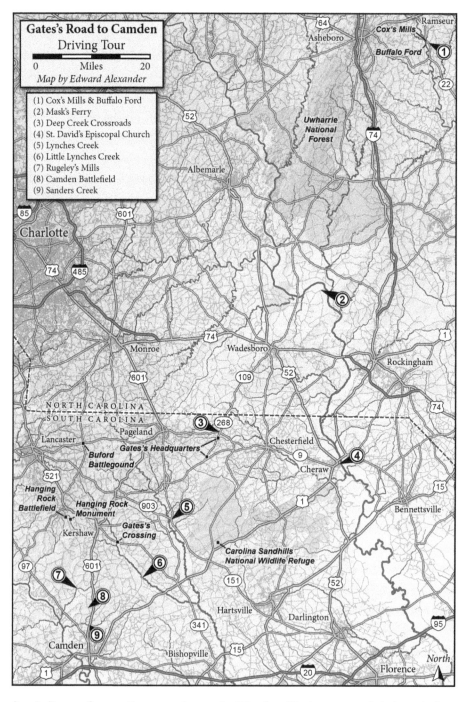

Gates's Road to Camden
Driving Tour

0   Miles   20

Map by Edward Alexander

(1) Cox's Mills & Buffalo Ford
(2) Mask's Ferry
(3) Deep Creek Crossroads
(4) St. David's Episcopal Church
(5) Lynches Creek
(6) Little Lynches Creek
(7) Rugeley's Mills
(8) Camden Battlefield
(9) Sanders Creek

GATES'S ROAD TO CAMDEN—Encompassing nearly 150 miles, this tour covers Gates's route from Buffalo Ford in North Carolina to Rugeley's Mills in South Carolina. Most stops are based on primary source materials, but the actual route between stops is mostly unknown. For this reason, driving directions are not provided but addresses and GPS coordinates are listed to assist you.

to help the American army in Charleston before it surrendered on May 12. De Kalb's men were under supplied and worn by many battles, and now a long march through Virginia and North Carolina forced de Kalb to stop his movement south. First, de Kalb encamped his forces at Wilcox's Iron Works (15 miles east of here) on July 6. Needing foodstuffs and to gather supplies, de Kalb began moving his command here to the Cox Mills/Buffalo Ford area a few weeks later.

Gates arrived here on the evening of July 24 and the next day held a meeting with his senior officers. After hearing from his officers and taking a quick look at the situation, Gates made the controversial decision to march his small force south on July 27. Gates believed the most direct route to Camden was preferable as he wanted to join with the North Carolina militia under Richard Caswell (as they had refused all entreaties to join the Continental forces at Deep River).

Nearby Buffalo Ford was the river crossing of the road from Hillsborough to Camden over Deep River.

Today, Buffalo Ford along Deep River is located near a modern highway bridge. This area was also home to Cox's Mills, which provided grain for the new Southern Army. The mill's foundations still exist off of NC Route 22 on private property. (ro)

The ford is 100 yards north of the highway bridge (located at GPS: 35°40'21.2"N 79°37'37.9"W). When de Kalb learned of Congress' appointment of Horatio Gates to take command of a reconstituted Southern Army, de Kalb knew this road would be an important route to consolidate forces. Cox's Mills were two mills run by the Cox family. They were located on Millstone Creek (located on NC 22 at GPS: 35°40'52.3"N 79°37'35.3"W). The main mill, run by Harmon Cox, was located to the north of the Millstone Creek bridge (the ruins are now on private property). Also, near here can be seen an original road trace of the Hillsborough—Camden Road.

Stop 2—Mask's Ferry

GPS: 35°06'06.2"N 79°56'00.6"W

The pull off is on the historic roadbed to Mask's Ferry (which is now on private property, about ½ mile away).

Gates's army were already short on rations and supplies, but now had to cross a mostly barren area of the Carolinas. Gates wrote, "the Desart (desert) affords Nothing, therefore the sooner we get through it the better." Gates set his men to march at a pace of 13 miles a day. They reached here at Mask's Ferry on the Pee Dee River on August 2. It took them several days to cross due to weather and flooding. Gates made his headquarters near here on the west side of the ferry. Gates also met here with Col. Charles Porterfield, who led a small contingent of 100 Virginia Light Infantry. Gates had previously detailed them to find cattle and foodstuffs for the army.

Gates was in constant communication with North Carolina militia general Richard Caswell. Gates was worried about the North Carolina militia and their forward position towards the British in South Carolina. Caswell to this point had refused every entreaty by de Kalb and Gates to move his men to join the Continental force. Now Gates was marching towards him to ensure their safety, and he believed they held supplies from the North Carolina government that could feed his own army. One force that Gates did not find necessary to keep with his army was that of the South Carolina partisan Francis Marion. Marion, dubbed the "Swamp Fox", led a small partisan force on horseback known for their black leather caps. His

This sandy roadway is the historic road trace that led to Mask's Ferry along the Pee Dee. This colonial era road was an important route for Indians and colonists as well as Gates's army as they headed south toward Camden. Though over 250 years old, witness trees of the past still remain today. (ro)

partisans were a mixture of white, black, and Native American men who were hard fighters. Gates saw little use for Marion and ordered him to work in the interior of South Carolina and to gather intelligence.

Before leaving Mask's Ferry, Gates issued a bold proclamation to the people of North and South Carolina. Gates assured the "real friends of America" that he was there to protect them and right the wrongs of the British occupiers. Their cause was the "cause of liberty" and Gates believed in the Divine providence of the American effort. He ended by stating, "The inhabitants of this state may rely on the assurance that an army composed of their brethren and fellow citizens cannot be brought among them with the hostile vices of plunder and depredation." Gates's men may not have been fully prepared for the campaign, but Gates's pen was fully capable.

Stop 3—Deep Creek Crossroads/ Little Black Creek Campsites

GPS: 34°46'10.3"N 80°13'35.6"W

The GPS coordinates are for a small parking lot at the Mt. Croghan Museum.

Gates's army entered into South Carolina north of here, near Thompson's Creek. In this area, labeled "Deep Creek Crossroads and Anderson's" in Gates's correspondence, the American army encamped from August 5-7. On August 6, Gates rode a few miles forward to meet with Caswell. He was shocked by how the officers were living in abundance. On August 6, the North Carolinian militia of 2,100 men joined Gates's army south of here. This lifted the confidence of the men as they began to look like a meaningful sized army. Though their struggles with supplies continued, and now Gates was responsible for feeding twice as many men.

It was obvious that the men in Gates's army were beginning to lose discipline, most likely due to their inability to get provisions and their steady marching in the extreme heat. Gates wrote in his orders on

It was near this crossroads, then known as Anderson's or Deep Creek Crossroads, that Gates encamped his army August 5-7, 1780. The Mt. Croghan Museum today interprets the history of this small rural community. (ro)

August 7, "The General hears with astonishment, the shameful Irregularity of the troops in straggling from Camp, and Marauding in a most Scandalous Manner, even stealing the Cloathing and Furniture of certain Inhabitants whom the Calamaties of War had already rendered but too miserable . . . . The First Soldier that is convicted of robbing and plundering the House of any Inhabitant shall suffer Death." Gates knew they were within a day's march (15 miles) of Rawdon's forces on the Lynches River, and soon every man would be expected to do his duty.

As you continue south on the old Camden Road (SC Rt. 268) you will cross two meaningful geographic landmarks that served as headquarters camp sites for Gates. The first will be Deep Creek, located at GPS: 34°45'22.1"N 80°13'53.3"W. The second is Little Black Creek located at GPS: 34°42'44.5"N 80°15'53.4"W. Both locations were used as camp sites and are mentioned in official orders from August 5-7.

Stop 4–Old St. David's Episcopal Church–Cheraw

GPS: 34°41'45.6"N 79°52'47.7"W

There is street parking at the location above and a pedestrian gate to the cemetery.

The original church building was built ca. 1770-1773 and is one of the few colonial church buildings standing in South Carolina. Later additions to the building were added in the 1800s. Saint David was the patron saint of Wales, the home of many Cheraw settlers. The church served as a hospital during the American Revolution and specifically the summer of 1780. In 1916, a new church was built nearby.

After the fall of Charleston, the British set up outposts across South Carolina at strategic points. At Cheraw Hills (modern day Cheraw), Cornwallis placed the 71st Regiment of Foot (Fraser's Highlanders). This allowed Rawdon in Camden to not only get an early warning if Gates approached, but also allowed him to spread out his units from disease-ridden Camden. These detachments also served to subdue uprisings and protect local Loyalists from Patriot partisans. The impact of the sickness that hit Cornwallis's army that summer cannot be overstated. Here the 71st Regiment of Foot suffered severely. The two battalions camped here along the Great Pee Dee River numbered around

Old St. David's Church in Cheraw, South Carolina, is one of the oldest standing churches in South Carolina. Built in 1770, it was the last Church of England built in South Carolina under King George III. In 1916, the church moved to another location in town and today the Chesterfield County Historic Preservation Commission owns the building. (ro)

300 men. Near the river in wet conditions in small huts and tents, the men were overcome with "fevers." The regimental surgeon noted that nearly all the men were impacted with sickness. When the 71st left Cheraw in late July, nearly 40 men were left behind due to their weakened condition.

Though little documentation exists from the 71st Regiment of Foot's records about burials, many diarists and locals of the time wrote about several of the British that died in the church and were buried in the church yard. There are several memorials in the church yard dedicated to the British buried here, one above a supposed officer's grave. Other graves are reportedly near the eastern vestry door and others on the south side of the church near the door.

Stop 5 – Lynches Creek

GPS: 34°33'56.1"N 80°22'02.6"W

This pull off at the intersection of SC 151 and SC 903 is approximately ¼ mile from Lynches Creek to the west.

Lord Rawdon, in command of the British forces in and around Camden, decided to not sit and wait for Gates to arrive but moved his forces to the western bank of Lynches Creek. Rawdon wrote his goal in moving here was "to retard the progress of Gates till Lord Cornwallis should collect force from other part of the Province, or to reduce the enemy to hazard an action where my peculiar advantages of situation would compensate for my disparity in numbers." It was this aggressiveness that made Gates worry about Caswell's forward position with his North Carolina militia. On August 8 Rawdon, believing that his outpost at Hanging Rock was defeated by Sumter (the news he received was exaggerated and the battle was a draw), decided to move back closer to Camden, to Little Lynches Creek a few miles west of Lynches Creek. This new position was supposedly a stronger defensive position.

The withdrawal of Rawdon from Lynches Creek gave Gates a false sense of confidence. Otho Holland Williams seemed to be more realistic in his synopsis that Rawdon "retired unmolested, and at leisure, to a much stronger position on Little Lynches Creek, within a days march of Camden." Before moving forward, Gates ordered his sickest men and heavy baggage north to Charlotte, though the large contingent of women and children still burdened the army. Gates was still hopeful the Virginia militia force promised by Governor Thomas Jefferson would join his army soon. This force of 700 militiamen was led by militia Brig. Gen. Edward Stevens and would bolster Gates's numbers. Gates's reliance on and trust of militia worked against him in the days ahead.

Rawdon's original position, and where Gates crossed the Lynches River, are not well documented. The main road from Deep Creek Crossroads came through here and there were several fords along the river here, the most prominent being Evans Ford.

Stop 6 – Little Lynches Creek

GPS: 34°25'44.4"N 80°27'10.2"W

There is a small pull off on the east side of the road and a private drive that goes down to Little Lynches Creek; this is private property so please do not trespass beyond the pull off and be cautious of highway traffic.

Though this stream is not very formidable, its banks are steep, and the bottom land area of Little Lynches Creek is about a mile wide. This marshy area made it very hard for any large force to cross, and provided a great barrier to the British force located on the heights south of here (the western bank).

Flush with confidence, Gates moved his force along the main road to Camden to Little Lynches Creek. There were not many places to cross Little Lynches; here there was a causeway built through the marsh for the main road. There were a few narrow places to cross, but those were still not easy crossings. Lord Rawdon established his main line on the heights above the creek with sentries posted along the creek itself. Rawdon described his position, "Lynches Creek runs thro swamps of perhaps a mile in breadth on each side; impenetrable, except where a causeway has been made at the passing places on the great road." It was a strong position, but Rawdon was outnumbered by Gates.

Gates sent Armand's Legion forward to feel out the British position. A small skirmish broke out with the only casualty being one of Armand's men captured. Post war accounts have certain officers in Gates's army encouraging him to attack (de Kalb being one), but most agreed the right move was to find a way around Rawdon. Unfortunately, this forced Gates to move his army northward approximately 6 miles around the British left flank, crossing Little Lynches Creek somewhere in the area around where

The steep banks along Little Lynches Creek as well as the vast wetlands in the bottom were a major obstacle for moving a large military force across the creek here. Lord Rawdon positioned the bulk of his army on the hills above the creek with a small force here along the water. A narrow causeway forced any force into a narrow area that could be easily attacked. (ro)

Hanging Rock Creek meets Little Lynches Creek (near a modern-day bridge across Little Lynches Creek at GPS: 34°30'44.4"N 80°31'27.1"W). Though Gates could easily cross Little Lynches Creek here, he would now be farther away from Camden. From this crossing, Gates determined to march westward to meet the Great Wagon Road at Rugeley's Mills. This road ran south from Rugeley's directly to Camden.

Stop 7—Rugeley's Mills

GPS: 34°24'08.8"N 80°38'30.8"W

There is no place to pull over and stop. These coordinates are for the bridge across Grannies Quarter Creek.

East of the bridge Col. Henry Rugeley, a local Tory, owned the plantation "Clermont." The mill was also located east of the bridge along Grannies Quarter Creek. Gates and his "Grand Army" arrived here on August 13. Gates was reinforced here by several hundred Virginia militia. These men were mostly inexperienced and equally undersupplied as Gates's army. Learning from Sumter that the British force in Camden was understrength, Sumter convinced Gates to send with him a few companies of Continentals and artillery. Sumter planned on going down the other side of the Wateree River to cut off the supply route from Ninety Six to Camden, as well as keep the British from retreating out of Camden towards Ninety Six.

Here Gates held his war council and made plans to move on Camden, even though his army proved to be much smaller than he expected. He ordered his army on a night march on August 15, their destination Sanders Creek. Gates ordered all extra wagons, baggage, and quartermaster stores to Waxhaws. Unfortunately, they were slow to leave and as the British followed up their victory at Camden, many of the wagons fell victim here to Tarleton's Legion.

Later in December 1780, a small fight took place here between Lt. Col. William Washington's American dragoons and Rugeley's Loyalist militia. Rugeley and his small force of 100 barricaded themselves into a "fort" Rugeley constructed out of his barn. The result was an American victory, with Rugeley surrendering and his self made "fort" destroyed by Washington.

Rugeley's Mills (or Clermont) sat on the eastern side of the road along Grannies Quarter Creek. Though nothing is left of the large industrial complex that was once here, this area is an important location in understanding the battle of Camden. Here Gates planned his next move toward the British in Camden. (dw)

Stop 8—Camden Battlefield

Author Mark Wilcox discusses with historians Rick Wise and Charles Baxley the positioning of the American line at Camden and how archaeology has helped identify the battle lines of both sides. (ro)

1698 Flat Rock Rd., Camden, SC 29090

Here the American and British armies clashed on the evening of August 15 and early morning of August 16. The American defeat here is one of the worst in U.S. history. The Camden battlefield is a great preservation success story. Overlooked by federal and state park preservation efforts, the battlefield has been preserved by a collaboration of local, state, and national history and environmental preservation organizations. Most of the preservation is recent, with a majority of the battlefield now preserved.

Today the park contains enhanced public access, new trails, and interpretive signage. The park covers the entire Camden campaign and puts the battle into context in the American Revolution, especially the Southern Campaign.

Stop 9—Sanders Creek (Saunders Creek)

GPS: 34°18'58.4"N 80°36'22.6"W

There is no place to pull over and stop. These coordinates are for the bridge across Sanders Creek.

This position along Sanders Creek was Gates's objective when he left Rugeley's Mills on the night of August 15. Notice the high elevation on the north side of the creek. This position was scouted out by engineer Col. John Christian Senf, along with Lieut. Col. Charles Porterfield. Gates's plan was to move his army here and use the terrain to hide his inexperienced militia, which comprised a majority of his army. Gates believed this position was strong and would force the British to either abandon Camden or attack him here. Unfortunately for Gates, the British moved faster than he expected.

This concludes the Gates's Route to Camden Tour. We recommend you continue into Camden to visit the Revolutionary War Visitor Center at Camden, 212 Broad St, Camden, SC 29020.

Saunders Creek today is mostly dammed up to form Colonial Lake to the east of the highway, but the high elevation that Gates sought after on the north bank is still easily apparent. It was here that Gates hoped to move his army and create a formidable defensive position. (ro)

BARON de KALB

Major General Johann de Kalb

"Sacred to the memory of Baron de Kalb, Knight of the Royal
Order of Military Merit, Brigadier of the Armies of France, and
Major General in the service of the United States of America ... he
gave a last and glorious proof of his attachment to the liberties of
mankind and the cause of America in the action near Camden in
the State of South Carolina on the sixteenth of August 1780 while
leading on the troops of Maryland and Delaware ... and animating
them by his example to deeds of valor ..."

Proclamation of the United States Congress, October 14, 1780

City of Camden Driving Tour

APPENDIX F

The city of Camden was founded in 1732 as the town of Fredericksburg. It was originally located further to the south of the current city near the Wateree River. Town leaders, including Joseph Kershaw, moved north to the area of Historic Camden and renamed it Pine Tree Hill. Kershaw pushed to have the town renamed Camden in honor of Lord Camden. Camden was a major trading and military post in the South Carolina back country. The city is one of the oldest inland settlements in South Carolina. In the twentieth century, Camden became known as a resort destination and center of the thoroughbred horse and steeplechase industry. Today, the city honors its history through various museums, historic sites, and an history interpretive trail throughout the town. This tour does not have to be followed in any order and some stops are within walking distance of each other. Other stops you will have to drive to. All are within the city of Camden proper.

Stop 1–Revolutionary War Visitor Center at Camden

212 Broad St., Camden, SC 29020

Opened in 2021, the Revolutionary War Visitor Center is a great place to orient yourself to the battle of Camden and also the multiple sites of the South Carolina Liberty Trail. The free exhibits provide background history to the Camden area and Revolutionary War events in the region. In 2022, a new statue honoring Baron de Kalb was unveiled in the courtyard. A retail store and restrooms are available.

Maj. Gen. Baron de Kalb is honored at many places across the country. In 2021, a new statue of de Kalb was dedicated at the Revolutionary War Center in Camden. (ro)

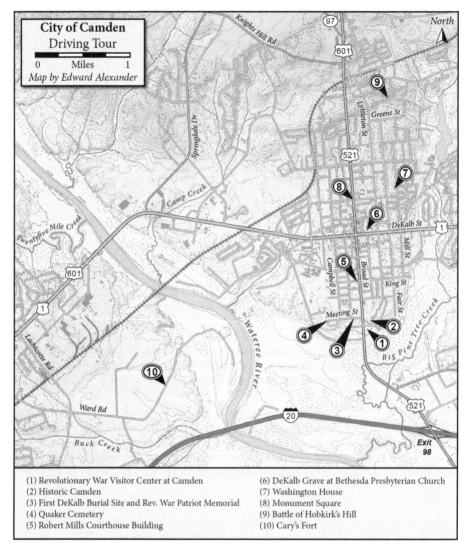

(1) Revolutionary War Visitor Center at Camden
(2) Historic Camden
(3) First DeKalb Burial Site and Rev. War Patriot Memorial
(4) Quaker Cemetery
(5) Robert Mills Courthouse Building
(6) DeKalb Grave at Bethesda Presbyterian Church
(7) Washington House
(8) Monument Square
(9) Battle of Hobkirk's Hill
(10) Cary's Fort

CITY OF CAMDEN DRIVING TOUR—The City of Camden is steeped in history and is very proud of its role in the American Revolution. The City of Camden Tour highlights significant historic sites in Camden that relate to the summer of 1780 and a few other Revolutionary War related sites. Your tour should begin at the Camden Revolutionary War Visitor Center.

Built in 2021, the Revolutionary War Visitor Center includes a museum, gift shop, meeting and rental space. It is a great introduction to the American Revolution in South Carolina and the perfect place to start your visit of Camden. (ro)

Stop 2—Historic Camden

222 Broad St., Camden, SC 29020

Historic Camden is a 107-acre outdoor museum complex that offers a view of life during colonial 19th century Camden. The site includes several historic structures that were preserved and moved here, and working living history areas including a blacksmith shop and brickyard. There is also the reconstructed Joseph Kershaw House, headquarters of Lord Cornwallis. The British occupation of Camden is interpreted through reconstructed palisade walls on original locations of the British palisade and redoubts.

Also on site is a 0.7-mile Nature Trail and picnic area. Local crafts, period reproductions, books, and other special gift selections are found in the museum gift shop. Special events and programs are offered year-round. There is a small admission fee, but this site is a great way to learn about Camden's early history and a fun place for people of all ages and interests.

Historic Camden is a 107-acre outdoor museum complex that interprets colonial and early American life in Camden and South Carolina. Highlighting original historic structures moved here and historic trades, Historic Camden provides a great interactive glimpse into the past. (ro)

Stop 3– First de Kalb Burial Site and Patriot Memorial

After succumbing to his many wounds at the nearby "Blue House" hospital on August 19th, de Kalb was placed in a grave here. Then President George Washington visited de Kalb's grave on his visit to Camden in May 1791. (ro)

GPS: 34°14'02.4"N 80°36'26.8"W

In this vicinity, within the British post, the Baron de Kalb was laid to rest. De Kalb was a well-respected military officer and was by all accounts treated well by Cornwallis and the British officers and doctors. De Kalb was moved from the battlefield to the "Blue House" hospital where he died on August 19. He was laid to rest in a grave with several British officers. The British gave him full military honors. Though a gravestone was present in 1811, a few years later an extensive investigation was required to find the original grave of de Kalb. This was part of the effort to move his body to a new location under a new monument. By 1825 his remains were found and moved from here to a new grave site in front of the Bethesda Presbyterian Church.

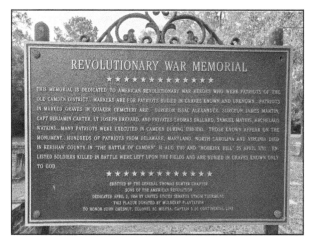

Located next to the Old Presbyterian Burying Ground, the Revolutionary War Memorial honors Patriots of Camden and others who died during the war while in Camden, including the battles of Camden and Hobkirk's Hill. (ro)

Across the street located next to the Old Presbyterian Burying Ground is the Revolutionary War Patriot Memorial. Dedicated in 1994, it honors American Patriots from Camden who fought in the war and those who suffered under British occupation. The memorial also honors the men that lost their lives at the battle of Camden and Hobkirk Hill. The first Presbyterian Meeting House (current Presbyterian church located on De Kalb Street) in Camden was also located here. Also, nearby is interpretive signage marking the location of the Southwest Redoubt of the British defenses of Camden. Along with the West Redoubt, this earthwork protected the western approach to Camden.

Stop 4—Quaker Cemetery

713 Meeting St., Camden, SC 29020

Established in 1759 as land set aside for a Quaker house of worship and burying ground, the cemetery today is now nearly 50 acres. Buried in this historic cemetery are many early nineteenth century Camden leaders and Civil War soldiers. Of special interest are some of the first Quaker burials that are now marked by long brick arches (early Quaker graves had no headstones). The cemetery today is a major historic and recreation spot in Camden.

Near the entrance of the Quaker Cemetery (it was located at the intersection of modern-day Campbell and Meeting Streets) was the location

Several reconstructed British redoubts are located around the Historic Camden campus, allowing visitors an opportunity to gain an understanding of the British defenses around Camden. (ro)

of the West Redoubt. This redoubt, along with the Southwest Redoubt, defended the western approach from the Wateree River to Camden. A nearby historic sign interprets the location of the redoubt.

Stop 5 — Robert Mills Courthouse Building

607 Broad St., Camden, SC 29020

This location was the site of the first courthouse in Camden. The structure that you see today was built ca. 1825 as a courthouse designed by South Carolinian architect Robert Mills (who also designed the de Kalb grave monument). The building has served as a courthouse, museum, archives, visitor center, municipal court, and a rental space.

Of special note behind the stairwell on the front of the building is an early grave marker for the Baron de Kalb. This stone is probably the stone referenced by Edwin Scott in 1811 when he noted that de Kalb's grave was "covered by a white stone slab, with an inscription eulogizing his character and services." The stone was found in the cellar of the Bethesda Presbyterian Church in 1901 and was moved here by the Hobkirk's Hill Chapter of the Daughters of the American Revolution.

Across Broad Street was the location of the jail. During the British occupation of Camden they kept

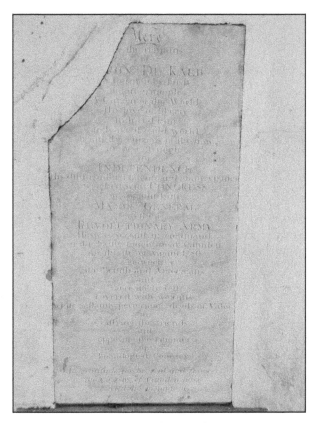

Located behind the front steps of the courthouse, the original grave stone for Baron de Kalb was found in the cellar of the Bethesda Presbyterian Church in 1911. This stone had marked de Kalb's grave at the corner of Church and Meeting Streets. (ro)

Patriot prisoners there, including future president Andrew Jackson who was a native of Waxhaws. Jackson was captured along with his brother in 1781. He was only 14 at the time of his capture. Jackson most likely was serving as a courier for the militia due to his young age. It was during this time in captivity that Jackson defied a British officer who demanded Jackson clean his boots. The officer struck Jackson, scarring his hand and forehead. The scars remained with Jackson his entire life and many say this fueled his negative view of the British later in his life.

Stop 6 – DeKalb Grave at Bethesda Presbyterian Church

502 E Dekalb St., Camden, SC 29020

In March 1825, DeKalb's remains were exhumed from his original burial site at Meeting Street and moved here in front of the Bethesda Presbyterian Church. Robert Mills, the designer of the Washington Monument, designed DeKalb's monument as well as the main church building. General LaFayette, a close friend of de Kalb, laid its cornerstone to much fanfare. Congress also authorized a monument to de Kalb soon after his death that is located in Annapolis, Maryland.

The first Bethesda Church was located near the location of the Old Presbyterian Burial Ground. This church was built in 1822 and designed by noted architect Robert Mills. The church went through many revisions but was returned to its original design in a 20th century restoration. (ro)

Stop 7 – Washington House

1413 Mill St., Camden, SC 29020
Private property, do not trespass.

This home was built in the 1780's and is the oldest house standing in Camden. The house was originally located at the corner of King and Fair Streets. It was here in May 1791 that leading citizens hosted President George Washington on his Southern Tour. Washington described Camden as "a small place with appearances of some new buildings." The house has been expanded several times since its construction.

Stop 8 – Monument Square

1314 Broad St., Camden, SC 29020

Monument Square contains several memorials, military monuments, and interpretive markers. Nearby is the site of the Camden Archives and Museum which preserves and exhibits the history of Camden, South Carolina and Kershaw County. The museum is a great place to learn about the history of the region and has an excellent genealogical library. This part of modern-day Camden was called "Logtown" in 1780, a small collection log buildings and houses.

The Camden Archives and Museum is the city history museum and research library. Exhibits highlight the entire history of Camden and Kershaw County. Admission is free. (ro)

Stop 9 – Battle of Hobkirk's Hill

GPS: 34°16'00.5"N 80°36'04.5"W

This small memorial park north of Camden is dedicated to the battle of Hobkirk's Hill, fought on April 25, 1781. Continental forces under Gen. Nathanael Greene positioned themselves on Hobkirk's Hill, threatening the British post at Camden under

Camden saw another major Revolutionary War battle on April 15, 1781 between Lord Rawdon and Nathaniel Greene's reconstituted Southern Army. Though a British victory, the British soon abandoned Camden to move back towards Charleston. Though today the battlefield is mostly developed, a series of interpretive markers through the neighborhood interpret the battle. (ro)

Lord Rawdon. Rawdon came out of Camden and attacked Greene. After a sharp fight, Greene withdrew from the hill, but a few weeks later Rawdon withdrew from Camden to Charleston. Though the hill is now covered in residential development, there are several interpretive markers along Hobkirk's Hill centered on Greene and Lyttleton Streets.

Stop 10—Cary's Fort

GPS: 34°13'26.2"N 80°38'31.7"W
Private property, do not trespass.

On the hill to your right (southeast) is the vicinity of Cary's Fort, established by Patriot-turned- Loyalist Lt. Col. James Cary. Cary built the fort on his own land on McCaa's Hill to protect the main ferry across the Wateree River into Camden. Cary posted an estimated 40 Loyalist militia inside the fort. On August 15, 1780 Col. Thomas Taylor of Sumter's

partisans attacked and captured the fort. Sumter's men also captured a relief column from Ninety Six heading to Camden that included supply wagons and 70 men of the 71st Regiment of Foot (Highlanders). The road you are on (Ward Rd.) dead ends just before the Wateree River. Near here was the river crossing into Camden.

Though the exact location of "Cary's Fort" is currently not known, it was in this general vicinity near the Wateree Ferry along the main road west out of Camden towards other British posts at Ninety Six and Augusta, GA. (ro)

The Camden Burial Project

APPENDIX G

MARK WILCOX

The battle of Camden, fought in the humid early morning hours of August 16, 1780, in South Carolina, was a nightmare for the Patriot forces engaged under the leadership of Maj. Gen. Horatio Gates. Facing an army of veteran British Regulars, Provincials, and Loyalist militia under the command of the brilliant Lt. Gen. Earl Cornwallis, the battle pitted the two largest British and Patriot forces in South Carolina against each other in an open pine forest north of the British occupied town of Camden.

For the Patriot army, the situation degenerated almost immediately. Within minutes of the opening shots of the battle, most of Gates's militia troops, mostly greenhorns from Virginia and North Carolina, panicked and fled in terror from the field. In their wake they left behind discarded muskets and other equipment strewn across the battlefield. Just moments into the fight, most of the left flank of the Patriot battle line was gone. On the right flank, across the Great Wagon Road that led to Camden, Gates's Continental troops, men and boys from Maryland and Delaware, soon found themselves virtually surrounded by the British and nearly annihilated. In less than an hour, the Southern American army was wrecked, leaving the way open for Lord Cornwallis to move his forces north, into North Carolina and Virginia.

Patriot losses at Camden were staggering, with nearly 3,000 killed, wounded, and captured. For the British, over 300 casualties were suffered, including several officers. Occupying the field after the battle, the British buried the dead of both armies in mostly shallow and hastily dug graves. For over 240 years, the remains of these veterans have lain almost undisturbed in these unmarked graves, presumably lost to history.

On September 19, 2022, a team of archaeologists and historians began a project to locate, excavate and recover the remains of some of these long-lost veterans of the battle of Camden. Led by archaeologist James

As part of the April 21, 2023, commemoration event, a funeral service was held for the 14 veterans recovered from the Camden battlefield. The service took place on the steps of Bethesda Presbyterian Church in the City of Camden. (mw)

Legg and scholar Dr. Steven Smith, both with the South Carolina Institute of Archeology and Anthropology (SCIAA), the project ultimately was able to excavate 7 grave features holding the remains of 14 veterans. The first discovery of remains occurred many years ago in the 1980's by relic hunters. Only about six acres of the battlefield had been preserved at that time, by the Daughters of the American Revolution. Most of the Camden battlefield site was commercially owned and unprotected back then. Today, over 800 acres of the battlefield have been saved and protected, now owned by the Historic Camden Foundation and the South Carolina Battleground Preservation Trust.

Initially envisioned on a modest scale, with Legg and Smith intending to excavate a limited number of grave sites with a small SCIAA crew, the Camden project team grew considerably over the course of nearly 8 weeks with the addition of numerous archaeologists and other professional individuals and volunteers from several agencies and organizations. According to Jim Legg, "Our small project became a major campaign." Of the 7 grave features examined, 4 were solitary graves while others held the remains of multiple individuals. The remains of 12 bodies from 5 of the grave features are believed to be Continental soldiers who fought in the area. Each set of remains had badly decayed pewter "USA" buttons which were indicative of the Continental regimental uniform coat, or other distinctively American diagnostic artifacts. Some grave features contained British .75 caliber round balls which, most likely, took the lives of the soldiers. According to James Legg, all the Continental graves "were irregular, and remarkably shallow with

During the battle of Camden, Continental troops from Maryland and Delaware fought under the direction of Baron de Kalb on the west side of the Great Wagon Road. The "USA" uniform buttons were typical of the Continental regimental coats worn by soldiers. (jl)

none more than 16 inches in depth." All the multiple burials were in shallow graves and too narrow for the occupants to lay side-by-side with remains "partially overlapping". Examination of the remains show that many of the Continentals were young, in their teens.

From the 14 burials, only one was determined to be the remains of a British soldier. He was an enlisted man of the 71st Regiment of Foot, Frasier's Highlanders. The 1st and 2nd Battalions of the 71st Regiment were engaged in the battle of Camden, on either side of the Great Wagon Road. According to Legg: "The 71st grave was the only reasonably formal burial we excavated. The individual was buried about two feet deep, in his uniform, neatly laid out in the conventional European grave posture with his hands over his waist." Due to the detail, it is believed this man was either buried by friends or at the direction of friends. From the grave of the Highlander, who was one of only 10 soldiers of the 71st killed in the battle, deteriorated pewter "71" buttons were recovered, along with the brass hardware from a 71st enlisted man's sword belt.

This .75 caliber British musket ball penetrated to the bone of the Patriot soldier and cracked it before coming to a rest. (jl)

Remains from the only other grave that may not have been a Continental soldier were recovered from one of the solitary burials. When the site was originally located years ago by relic hunters, among the artifacts found were indiscriminate civilian pewter buttons of the period. The position of the grave on

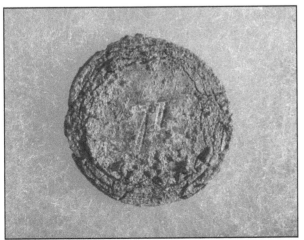

This is a pewter uniform button recovered from the grave of an enlisted man in the 71st Regiment of Foot, known as Fraser's Highlanders. There were two battalions of the 71st Regiment fighting at Camden on both sides of the Great Wagon Road. (jl)

Having the 71st regimental device, this brass hardware is from the standard issue shoulder sword belt of an enlisted man in the 71st Regiment of Foot, Fraser's Highlanders. The sword belt was lying on top of the soldier's remains rather than worn by him. (jl)

the battlefield, on the extreme left flank of the British, possibly suggests this man was serving with the North Carolina Loyalist militia who were engaged with the Continentals in the area. This individual was buried face-down in an irregular, shallow grave. His remains had also been disturbed by farmers plowing their field. Probably the most remarkable feature of the man buried here was discovered when his skull was examined in a lab. His teeth suggest he was most likely of Native American ancestry. According to Jim Legg, this put a new light on what to do with these remains. "This development, of course, led immediately to a consultation with appropriate Native American authorities, who provided requirements for the treatment and disposition of the soldier's remains. No DNA, isotopic, or other samples will be removed from the individual and we have specific directions regarding this reburial."

In April 2023, the culmination of the project centered around a major commemorative event in the City of Camden which was planned and hosted by the Historic Camden Foundation and the South Carolina Battleground Preservation Trust. With full military honors, the remains of the 14 individuals who were recovered from the battlefield were placed in coffins that were specially made from wood at the Historic Camden Revolutionary War Site. There the veterans laid in state in the Kershaw House where public visitation was allowed. On Saturday, April 21, townspeople, visitors, and living historians gathered at Bethesda Presbyterian Church in Camden where, on the front steps of the church, a funeral service was held for the battlefield veterans. It is also here, in the church yard, where a monument stands over the final resting place of Maj. Gen. Johann, Baron de Kalb, one of the key figures in the Patriot effort at the battle of Camden. The cornerstone of the monument was laid in March 1825 by the aging Marquis de Lafayette.

With the funeral service concluded, the veterans were returned to the battlefield where they were commemorated by public officials of the state of South Carolina, including Governor Henry McMaster. Military honor guards from the United

On April 21, 2023, a United States Military Honor Guard escorted the flagged-draped coffins holding the remains of the Continental soldiers that were excavated and recovered on the Camden battlefield in September 2022. (mw)

As part of the Camden commemoration on April 21, 2023, a United Kingdom Military Honor Guard escorts the remains of the only British soldier recovered from the battlefield in September 2022. This soldier was an enlisted man in the 71st Regiment of Foot. (jl)

States and United Kingdom solemnly conducted the veterans back to the field where they fought and died over 200 years ago. Also, in recognition of the roles played in the Southern American army by Baron de Kalb and Lt. Col. Charles Armand, representatives of the German and French militaries were likewise on hand for the event. Volunteers, local living historians portraying Patriots and Redcoats, and hundreds of visitors turned out for the commemoration.

Originally, the project called for the 14 veterans to be reburied on the battlefield with honors, in the grave sites where they were recovered. Deemed unacceptable by the United States Military, negotiations continue in determining the most appropriate location for where these heroes will lie. Whether in an established cemetery in Camden or in one to be created by the military, these veterans who laid in unmarked graves for over two centuries, many of them young men, will at last have the chance to rest in peace in properly marked sites.

United States Military Honor Guard removing the American flags from the coffins of the Patriot veterans recovered from the Camden battlefield. As part of the commemoration ceremony, each flag was folded and presented to honorary pallbearers from Camden. (mw)

Living historians portraying Patriot soldiers turned out in droves for the commemoration ceremony held at the Camden battlefield on April 21, 2023. (mw)

The Camden battlefield is one of the best preserved battlefields of the American Revolution. Its preservation is due to a large group of historians, preservationists, and conservationists who have worked hard to preserve this hallowed ground. (ro)

Today, the flags of South Carolina, Virginia, and the United States fly over the Waxhaws Battlefield, reflecting the historic connection between the two states. (ro)

THE BATTLE OF CAMDEN

CROWN FORCES
Lt. Gen. Charles Lord Cornwallis

British Regular Troops Lt. Col. James Webster
16th Regiment of Foot (light infantry only) • 23rd Regiment of Foot
(Royal Welch Fusiliers) • 33rd Regiment of Foot • 71st Regiment of Foot
(Fraser's Highlanders)

Royal Artillery
3rd Battalion • 4th Battalion

Provincial Troops Col. Francis Lord Rawdon
British Legion • Volunteers of Ireland • Royal North Carolina Regiment
Loyalist North Carolina Militia

CONTINENTAL FORCES
Maj. Gen. Horatio Gates

DE KALB'S DIVISION Maj. Gen. Baron De Kalb
Smallwood Maryland Brigade Brig. Gen. William Smallwood
1st Maryland • 3rd Maryland • 5th Maryland • 7th Maryland

Gist Maryland–Delaware Brigade Brig. Gen. Mordecai Gist
2nd Maryland • 4th Maryland • 6th Maryland • 1st Delaware Regiment
(6 companies)

Armand's Legion of Cavalry and Infantry Lt. Col. Charles Tuffin Armand
1st Troop Dragoons • 2nd Troop Dragoons • 3rd Troop Dragoons
German Infantry Volunteers • Chasseur Infantry Company
South Carolina Volunteer Mounted Infantry • Virginia State Cavalry

Continental Artillery Col. Charles Harrison
1st Continental Maryland Artillery • 2nd Continental Maryland Artillery
3rd Continental Maryland Artillery • 1st Continental Virginia Artillery

Light Infantry Maj. John Armstrong
Lt. Col. Porterfield's Virginia State Militia Light Infantry
Maj. John Armstrong's North Carolina State Militia Light Infantry

North Carolina Militia Brig. Gen. Richard Caswell
Butler Brigade Brig. Gen. John Butler
Caswell County Militia • Northampton County Militia • Orange County Militia
Randolph County Militia • Wake County Militia

Rutherford Brigade Brig. Gen. Griffith Rutherford
Lincoln County Militia • Mecklenburg County Militia • Rowan County Militia
Surry County Militia

Gregory Brigade Brig. Gen. Isaac Gregory
Caswell County Militia • Craven County Militia • Franklin County Militia
Orange County Militia • Rowan County Militia • Warren County Militia
Yarborough's North Carolina Continental Veterans

Virginia Militia Brig. Gen. Edward Stevens
Amelia County Militia • Amherst County Militia • Bedford County Militia
Caroline County Militia • Charlotte County Militia • Chesterfield County Militia
Culpeper County Militia • Dinwiddie County Militia • Fauquier County Militia
Hanover County Militia • Halifax County Militia • Henry County Militia
Louisa County Militia • Lunenburg County Militia • Mecklenburg County
Militia • Pittsylvania County Militia • Powhatan County Militia

Various South Carolina Militia

THE BATTLE OF CAMDEN

De Kalb: One of the Revolutionary War's Bravest Generals
John Beakes
Heritage Books, 2019
ISBN: 978-0788459009

A great biography on de Kalb with a heavy reliance
on primary sources. Beakes focuses several chapters
on de Kalb's role in the Southern campaign. Includes
information on de Kalb's burial, burial sites, modern
connections to de Kalb, and other interesting
appendices on de Kalb and his family (military and
personal).

*The Road to Guilford Courthouse: The American Revolution
in the Carolinas*
John Buchanan
University of Michigan, 1997
ISBN: 978-1620456026

Buchanan's work is a great introduction to the
Southern campaign of the Revolutionary War. Easy
to read, Buchanan follows the campaign from the
battle of Sullivan's Island in 1776 up to the battle
of Guilford Courthouse in 1781. It contextualizes
the actions around Charleston within the partisan
fighting that broke out in the backcountry between
the fall of Charleston and the battle at Guilford.

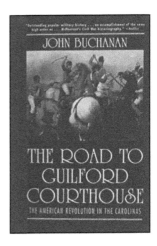

Horatio Gates and the Battle of Camden: "That Unhappy Affair," August 16, 1780
John Maass
Kershaw County Historical Society, 2001
ISBN: 978-1931799003

A well-researched and concise booklet on the battle of Camden, Gates's leadership, and strategic decisions. Maass addresses some of the misconceptions of Gates during the battle and post battle views of his performance.

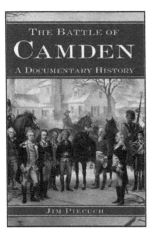

The Battle of Camden: A Documentary History
Jim Piecuch
History Press, 2006
ISBN: 978-1596291447

Dr. Piecuch's work is not a typical narrative history, but an accumulation of select primary sources of contemporaries and combatants on both sides. It is a great resource for anyone interested in Camden and the American Revolution and a must have for anyone studying the Southern campaign.

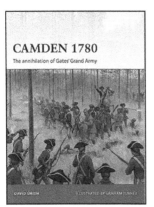

Camden 1780: The annihilation of Gates' Grand Army
David Smith
Osprey Publishing, 2016
ISBN: 978-1472812858

The most recent study on the battle of Camden, Smith provides the actions in Camden in context in the Southern campaign of 1780. Beginning with the fall of Charleston, his narrative covers all the events leading up to Camden, including detailed accounts of Waxhaws and partisan fighting in the summer of 1780. The work also includes full-color maps and artistic renditions of scenes from the battle, a staple of the Osprey series.

Nothing but Blood and Slaughter: The Revolutionary War in the Carolinas, Volume Two, 1780
Patrick O'Kelley
Booklocker.com, Inc., 2004
ISBN: 978-1591135883

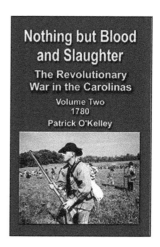

A comprehensive listing of all the military actions (land and naval) in South Carolina in four volumes. Each skirmish/battle includes a comprehensive, easy-to-understand narrative history, order of battle, and casualty lists.

Parker's Guide to the Revolutionary War in South Carolina
John Parker
Infinity Publishing, 2014
ISBN: 978-0741499417

One of the most comprehensive guidebooks on the American Revolution in South Carolina, Parker attempts to document every military action in South Carolina, with GPS coordinates and a description of what remains at each site. Parker includes maps and little-known details that make having his work valuable while seeking out Revolutionary War sites within South Carolina.

Unhappy Catastrophes

The American Revolution in Central New Jersey, 1776–1782

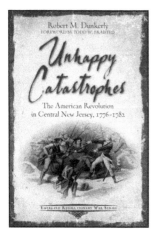

"The Importance of the North River (the Hudson), and the sanguine wishes of all to prevent the enemy from possessing it, have been the causes of this unhappy catastrophe." So wrote General George Washington in 1776 as the British invaded New Jersey. Worse was to come, as the British overran the state, and the Americans suffered one unhappy catastrophe after another.

Central New Jersey witnessed many small battles and important events during the American Revolution. This area saw it all: from spies and espionage, to military encampments like Morristown and Middlebrook, to mutinies, raids, and full-blown engagements like Bound Brook, Short Hills, and Springfield. The British had their own catastrophes too. So did civilians caught in the middle.

In the fall of 1776, British forces drove the Americans out and secured the state. Following the battles of Trenton and Princeton, New Jersey became a battleground. The spring of 1777 saw the formation of a new Continental Army, one that served the rest of the war. That spring, British and American forces clashed in a series of small but sharp battles. By summer, British General Howe tried to lure Washington into a major engagement, but the Americans avoided the trap. As the conflict dragged on, civilians became engulfed in the fray, and a bitter civil war erupted, continuing until the end of the conflict.

In *Unhappy Catastrophes: The American Revolution in Central New Jersey, 1776–1782*, Robert M. Dunkerly follows the course of the war through its various phases and details lesser-known battles, military campsites, raids, espionage, and more. The book also includes historic sites to visit, markers, and websites for further research and study. This part of New Jersey saw more action during the Revolution than anywhere else in the young nation and has been called the Cockpit of the Revolution. To truly understand the war, look at central New Jersey.

The Winter that Won the War

The Winter Encampment at Valley Forge, 1777–1778

"An Army of skeletons appeared before our eyes naked, starved, sick and discouraged."

Gouverneur Morris recorded these words in his report to the Continental Congress after a visit to the Continental Army encampment at Valley Forge. Sent as part of a fact-finding mission, Morris and his fellow congressmen arrived to conditions far worse than they had initially expected.

After a campaigning season that saw the defeat at Brandywine, the loss of Philadelphia, the capital of the rebellious British North American colonies, and the reversal at Germantown, George Washington and his harried army marched into Valley Forge on December 19, 1777.

What transpired in the next six months prior to the departure from the winter cantonment on June 19, 1778 was truly remarkable. The stoic Virginian, George Washington solidified his hold on the army and endured political intrigue, the quartermaster department was revived with new leadership from a former Rhode Island Quaker, and a German baron trained the army in the rudiments of being a soldier and military maneuvers.

Valley Forge conjures up images of cold, desperation, and starvation. Yet Valley Forge also became the winter of transformation and improvement that set the Continental Army on the path to military victory and the fledgling nation on the path to independence.

In *The Winter that Won the War: The Winter Encampment at Valley Forge, 1777-1778*, historian Phillip S. Greenwalt takes the reader on campaign in the year 1777 and through the winter encampment, detailing the various changes that took place within Valley Forge that ultimately led to the success of the American cause. Walk with the author through 1777 and into 1778 and see how these months truly were the winter that won the war.

A Handsome Flogging

The Battle of Monmouth, June 28, 1778

June 1778 was a tumultuous month in the annals of American military history. Somehow, General George Washington and the Continental Army were able to survive a string of defeats around Philadelphia in 1777 and a desperate winter at Valley Forge. As winter turned to spring, and spring turned to summer, the army—newly trained by Baron von Steuben and in high spirits thanks to France's intervention into the conflict—marched out of Valley Forge in pursuit of Henry Clinton's British Army making its way across New Jersey for New York City.

What would happen next was not an easy decision for Washington to make. Should he attack the British column? And if so, how? "People expect something from us and our strength demands it," Gen. Nathanael Greene pressed his chieftain. Against the advice of many of his subordinates, Washington ordered the army to aggressively pursue the British and not allow the enemy to escape to New York City without a fight.

On June 28, 1778, the vanguard of the Continental Army under Maj. Gen. Charles Lee engaged Clinton's rearguard near the small village of Monmouth Court House. Lee's over-cautiousness prevailed and the Americans were ordered to hasty retreat. Only the arrival of Washington and the main body of the army saved the Americans from disaster. By the end of the day, they held the field as the British continued their march to Sandy Hook and New York City.

In *A Handsome Flogging: The Battle of Monmouth, June 28, 1778*, historian William Griffith retells the story of what many historians have dubbed the "battle that made the American army," and takes you along the routes trekked by both armies on their marches toward destiny. Follow in the footsteps of heroes (and a heroine) who, on a hot summer day, met in desperate struggle in the woods and farm fields around Monmouth Court House.

Victory or Death

The Battles of Trenton and Princeton, December 25, 1776–January 3, 1777

December 1776: Just six months after the signing of the Declaration of Independence, George Washington and the new American Army sit on the verge of utter destruction by the banks of the Delaware River. The despondent and demoralized group of men had endured repeated defeats and now were on the edge of giving up hope. Washington feared "the game is pretty near up."

Rather than submit to defeat, Washington and his small band of soldiers crossed the ice-choked Delaware River and attacked the Hessian garrison at Trenton, New Jersey, on the day after Christmas. He followed up the surprise attack with successful actions along the Assunpink Creek and at Princeton. In a stunning military campaign, Washington had turned the tables, and breathed life into the dying cause for liberty during the Revolutionary War.

The campaign has led many historians to deem it as one of the most significant military campaigns in American history. One British historian even declared that "it may be doubted whether so small a number of men ever employed so short a space of time with greater or more lasting results upon the history of the world."

In *Victory or Death*, historian Mark Maloy not only recounts these epic events, he takes you along to the places where they occurred. He shows where Washington stood on the banks of the Delaware and contemplated defeat, the city streets that his exhausted men charged through, and the open fields where Washington himself rode into the thick of battle. Victory or Death is a must for anyone interested in learning how George Washington and his brave soldiers grasped victory from the jaws of defeat.

About the Authors

Robert Orrison is co-founder of Emerging Revolutionary War and has worked in the public history field for over 25 years. He currently serves as the Division Manager for the Prince William County (VA) Office of Historic Preservation. Some of his published works include *A Single Blow: The Battles of Lexington and Concord and the Beginning of the American Revolution*; *A Want of Vigilance: The Bristoe Station Campaign*; *The Last Road North: A Guide to the Gettysburg Campaign, 1863*; and *To Hazard All: A Guide to the Maryland Campaign, 1862*.

Mark Wilcox is an historian who currently works as a ranger at Richmond National Battlefield Park and the Maggie L. Walker National Historic Site, leading battlefield tours around Richmond and presenting programs on the city's Revolutionary War, Civil War, and Civil Rights history. He is the published author of the historic fiction work *Autumnfield*. Mark is also a living historian of the Colonial era who has provided educational programs for many public historic sites in Virginia. He is a member of the Richmond Chapter of the Revolutionary War Roundtable and blogs for Emerging Revolutionary War.